DINING
IN STYLE

DINING IN STYLE

Creating and Presenting Memorable Meals for Elegant Entertaining, Special Occasions and Festive Holidays

ARCH CAPE PRESS
New York

CONTENTS

Recipes Edited by Judith Ferguson
Photography by Michael Boys
Introduction by Pam Boys

CLB 2259
© 1989 Colour Library Books Ltd., Godalming, Surrey, England.
© Illustrations: Michael Boys Syndication, England.
Colour separations by Hong Kong Graphic Arts Ltd., Hong Kong.
Printed and bound in Italy by New Interlitho.
This edition published 1989 by Arch Cape Press, a division of dilithium Press, Ltd.
Distributed by Crown Publishers, Inc., 225 Park Avenue South, New York, New York 10003.
ISBN 0 517 68137 4
h g f e d c b a

INTRODUCTION

From simple yet unusual appetizers to sophisticated gourmet dishes, *Dining in Style* is both a culinary inspiration as well as a visual joy. Leaf through these pages and you will find food ideas to suit every conceivable occasion; from robust dishes for cold winter evenings to delicate fare that would grace the most elegant dinner party spread. With a wealth of recipes complemented by the superb photography of Michael Boys, here is a cookbook that can offer something for everyone.

A chapter on delicate dishes brings together subtle ideas for the fastidious appetite, while the seafood section tempts the palate with its mouthwatering ideas and stunning presentations. The weight watcher, too, will discover novel salad ideas that taste just as good as they look.

For those long, lazy summer days there are hints that will turn an everyday picnic or barbecue into a novel experience. Sandwiches, too, get a lift, with original flavors and tempting fillings providing a refreshing change from those tired, everyday varieties.

If it's poultry or meat that you are preparing, then turn to the relevant chapter and see just what can be done with lamb, duck and even pigeon, and even if you don't follow the recipe to the letter it will inspire you to experiment with different flavor combinations.

Mushrooms, somewhat unusually, are given individual treatment that encourages the reader to experiment with this versatile food, while the chapter on vegetable fare provides a multitude of hints for tasty accompaniments.

What more enjoyable way can there be of spending an evening with friends than around a table enjoying good food, fine wine and lively conversation? Entertaining Dishes presents a host of ideas on elegant party fare, while chapters on Fruit Fantasies and Indulgent Desserts provide a wealth of tempting ideas on how to round off the perfect meal.

Facing page: PINEAPPLE COCONUT ROLL.

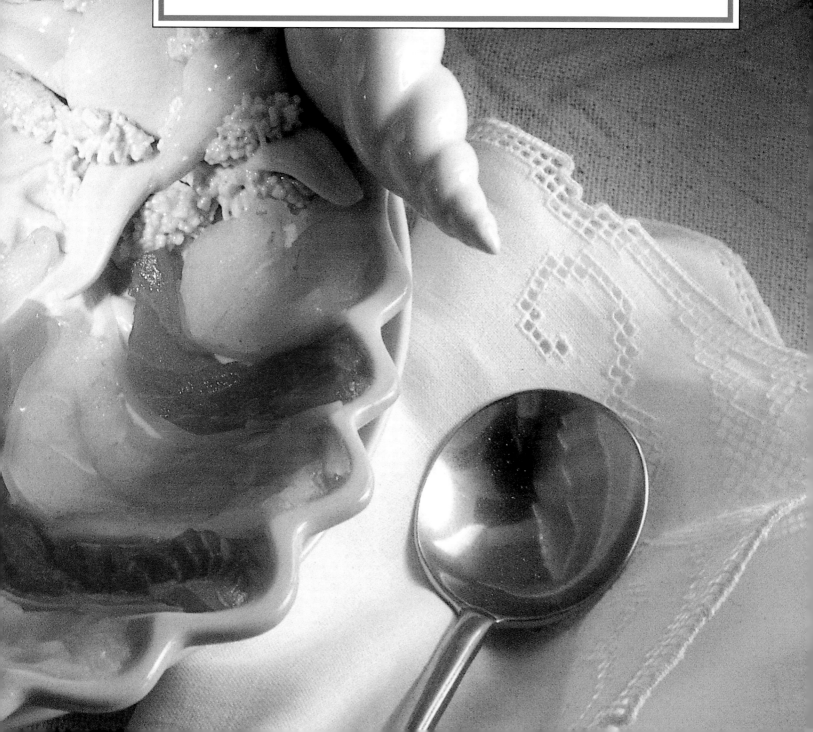

Chapter 1

ELEGANT APPETIZERS

NESTS OF QUAIL'S EGGS AND SHRIMP

Lightly cooked leeks form the 'nests' for quail's eggs and shrimp in this unusual appetizer. It can double as a main course salad, too.

INGREDIENTS

6 leeks, trimmed and washed □ 4 tbsps oil □ 1½ tbsps lime juice □ Pinch cayenne pepper and sugar □ 1 hard-boiled egg □ 8 quail's eggs, hard-boiled □ 4oz cooked and peeled shrimp □ Parsley and sliced limes to garnish

---

Cook the leeks whole in boiling salted water until barely tender. Drain well and cut in half lengthwise. Mix the oil, lime juice, cayenne and sugar and pour over the leeks. Marinate 1–2 hours.

Twist the leeks into circles and place 3 on each serving plate. Quarter the hard-boiled egg and place 1 quarter in a circle.

Quarter 4 of the quail's eggs and leave 4 whole. Arrange 4 whole quail's eggs in another circle and surround with the quartered eggs. Fill the remaining circle with shrimp. Spoon over any remaining dressing from the leeks and serve.

GOLDEN FLOUNDER SOUP WITH FRESH FISH GARNISH

Very thinly sliced fish 'cooks' in the hot soup, tinted golden with saffron. For this soup, fresh fish is absolutely essential.

Previous page: GOLDEN FLOUNDER SOUP
WITH FRESH FISH GARNISH
Facing page: NEST OF QUAIL'S EGGS AND SHRIMP.

INGREDIENTS
---

4 tbsps butter or margarine □ 1 small onion, finely chopped □ 1 large carrot, chopped □ 1 stick celery, chopped □ 1 potato, peeled and diced □ ½ tsp freshly grated ginger □ 1lb flounder fillets, skinned □ 3 cups water □ 1 cup dry white wine □ Large pinch saffron □ Salt and white pepper □ 1½ cups heavy cream

---
GARNISHES
---

1 leek, well washed and shredded □ 4oz halibut fillets, skinned and thinly sliced □ 4oz salmon fillets, skinned and thinly sliced

---

Melt the butter in a large saucepan, add the onion, carrot, celery and potato and cook slowly to soften without coloring. Add the ginger, flounder, water, wine, saffron and seasoning. Bring to the boil and then simmer for 20–25 minutes, or until the fish is cooked and the vegetables are soft. Pour the soup into a food processor or blender and purée until smooth. Sieve, if desired.

Blanch the leek shreds in boiling water for 1 minute and drain well. Place the slices of fish in serving bowls along with the leek shreds. Reheat the soup, add the cream and bring to the boil. Ladle the hot soup over the fish and leeks and serve immediately.

SERVES 4

SMOKED FISH IN LETTUCE PARCELS

Roulades of creamy smoked fish pâté and crisp lettuce can serve as a first course, a cocktail savory or a marvelous snack.

INGREDIENTS
---

2 smoked mackerel fillets □ 1 tsp horseradish □ 2 tsp chopped fresh dill □ 4oz cream cheese □ 1 tbsp lemon juice □ 1 round or Webb lettuce, washed

---

Skin the smoked mackerel and remove any bones. Break up the fish and place it in a food processor with the horseradish, dill, cream cheese and lemon juice. Process until smooth.

Separate the lettuce leaves and discard any discolored or blemished ones. Blanch the rest in boiling water for about 20 seconds. Drain, rinse under cold water and pat dry.

Divide the mixture evenly and place one portion on each lettuce leaf. Form the mixture into a sausage shape and roll up the lettuce leaf around it. Continue with the remaining mixture and leaves.

Place close together in a shallow dish, seam side down, and chill for at least 30 minutes to firm up. Use any leftover lettuce to garnish the serving plate, and place the parcels on top.

SERVES 8–10

PARSNIPS AND PASTRY

Parsnips in an appetizer make it unusual. A chicory sauce is even more so, but the combination is a highly successful one. Crispy pastry provides a contrast of texture.

―――――――――― INGREDIENTS ――――――――――

8oz puff pastry □ 1 egg beaten with a pinch of salt □ 3 medium-sized chicory (Belgian endive), washed □ 4 tbsps butter or margarine □ Salt and pepper □ 1 cup stock □ Pinch sugar (optional) □ 1 cup heavy cream □ Pinch mace □ 6 medium-sized parsnips, peeled

―――――――――――――――――――――――――――――――

Roll out pastry to ¼ inch thickness. Cut out 6 rectangles. Place them on a dampened baking sheet and brush with the egg and salt glaze. Bake at 425°F for 10–15 minutes until risen and browned. Keep warm.

Melt the butter or margarine in a saucepan. Remove the chicory cores and slice the leaves very thinly. Cook slowly in the butter or margarine until beginning to soften. Add salt and pepper and pour on the stock. Simmer until barely tender. Taste and add sugar if necessary. Add the cream and simmer 10 minutes to thicken. Add the mace.

Meanwhile, slice the parsnips thinly and steam over simmering water for about 5–6 minutes or until tender. Place a rectangle of pastry on each plate with some parsnips. Spoon chicory sauce over the parsnips to serve.

PINK TROUT MOUSSE WITH SORREL SAUCE

Sorrel is a herb with a leaf very much like that of spinach. It has a slightly lemony taste and is excellent with fish.

INGREDIENTS

10oz salmon trout, skinned and boned □ 1 cup fromage frais (8% fat variety) □ 1 egg □ 1½ tbsps butter □ Salt and pepper □ Oil □ 4 tbsps butter □ 4oz sorrel, finely chopped □ 1½ cups heavy cream □ Dash lemon juice □ Chives, chervil and red caviar to garnish

---

Place the fish in a food processor and work to a purée. Add the fromage frais, egg, butter and seasoning and work until smooth. Oil 4 ramekin dishes or small molds and spoon in the trout mixture. Cover each with a piece of oiled foil. Place in a roasting pan with enough hot water to come halfway up the sides of the dishes or molds.

Place in a 400°F oven and cook about 30 minutes or until a skewer inserted into the center comes out clean. Leave in the hot water to keep warm.

Melt the butter in a saucepan and add the sorrel. Cook for about 5 minutes and pour in 1 cup heavy cream. Bring to the boil, then simmer a few minutes to thicken. Add seasoning to taste and a little lemon juice.

To serve, spoon the sauce onto plates and unmold the mousses. Place them on top of the sauce. Use the remaining cream to spoon around the mousses. Garnish with chives, chervil leaves and red caviar. Serve warm.

SERVES 4

Facing page: PINK TROUT MOUSSE WITH SORREL SAUCE.

Elegant Appetizers

CHICORY SUNFLOWER

Dips for raw vegetables are increasingly popular and perfect for a busy cook to prepare. This arrangement can give your party a sunny look anytime of the year.

--- INGREDIENTS ---

1 ripe avocado, pitted and peeled □ 2 tbsps toasted sunflower seeds □ 6 tbsps low fat soft cheese □ 1 tbsp lemon juice □ Salt and pepper □ 4 heads chicory (Belgian endive) □ Fresh basil or mint leaves for garnishing

Purée the avocado in a food processor. Add the sunflower seeds and process to chop finely. Process in the soft cheese, lemon juice, salt and pepper. Spoon into a serving bowl and cover.

Remove the cores from the chicory and separate the leaves. Place the bowl of avocado mixture in the center of a round serving plate and arrange the chicory leaves around it like petals. Garnish with fresh herbs.

LOBSTER SOUP PRIMAVERA

A rich, creamy soup with a taste of spring vegetables makes a fantastic first course that is well worth the preparation.

--- INGREDIENTS ---

1½lbs potatoes □ 1 cup milk □ ½ cup fish stock □ ⅓ cup heavy cream □ 2 cooked lobsters □ 8oz assorted spring vegetables (baby carrots, lima beans, asparagus tips, zucchini, cherry tomatoes) □ Salt and white pepper □ Chervil sprigs

Facing page: CHICORY SUNFLOWER.

16

Peel and dice the potatoes. Place in a large saucepan with the milk and stock. Cover and bring to the boil. Simmer until the potatoes are tender. Purée in a food processor and sieve, if desired.

Crack the lobster tails and claw shells and extract the meat. Save the heads and small legs for garnishing, if desired. Chop the meat and add to the soup. Season to taste.

Prepare the vegetables and blanch all but the tomatoes in boiling water for a few minutes, or until just tender. Spoon the soup into bowls and garnish with an assortment of vegetables and sprigs of chervil.

SERVES 4

CRAB MEAT IN CUCUMBER CUPS

Seafood and cucumbers go well together, and crab meat is an especially good choice. Salting cucumbers first will keep the dish from becoming watery.

INGREDIENTS
---

1 cucumber □ 4oz crab meat □ ¼ tsp Dijon mustard □ Pinch salt and cayenne pepper □ 2 tbsps mayonnaise

---

Choose an unblemished cucumber with a straight shape. Cut off both ends and then use a cannelle knife to score strips through the peel. Cut into 1-inch-thick rounds. Use a small melon baller to scoop out the center of each slice to form cups.

Sprinkle the scooped out centers and the cups lightly with salt and leave to stand for 30 minutes to drain. Rinse well and pat dry. Chop the scooped-out cucumber finely.

Mix the chopped cucumber with the crab meat, mustard, salt, cayenne and mayonnaise. Fill the cucumber cups with the mixture, mounding it up slightly on top. Chill briefly before serving.

SERVES 8–10

Facing page: CRAB MEAT IN CUCUMBER CUPS.

SMOKED SALMON AND SPINACH SPIRALS

*Gravad Laks is a popular Scandinavian first course and this is a variation on that theme.
Using smoked salmon instead of fresh shortens the marinating time.*

--- INGREDIENTS ---

8oz sliced smoked salmon □ 8oz fresh spinach □ Chopped fresh dill □ Sugar,
allspice and white pepper □ 1½ cups sour cream □ 1 tbsp mild Swedish
mustard □ 2 tsps white wine vinegar □ 3 tomatoes, peeled and
seeded □ Watercress leaves

Lay out the slices of smoked salmon on a clean work surface slightly overlapping them.

Wash the spinach well and remove the stems and center rib. Cover the top of the salmon with the spinach. Sprinkle with fresh dill and a pinch of sugar, allspice and white pepper. Roll up the salmon like a jelly roll and wrap in plastic wrap. Refrigerate for several hours for the flavors to blend.

Reserve about 6 tbsps of the sour cream and combine the remainder with the mustard in a food processor. Stir in the vinegar and add a pinch of sugar to balance the taste.

Cut 1 tomato in short strips and chop the others finely. Add the chopped tomatoes to the food processor and purée until the sauce is an even color.

Spoon the sauce onto serving plates, tilting them to spread the sauce evenly. Slice the salmon roll into 12 slices and place 3 on each plate on top of the sauce.

Mix the reserved sour cream until smooth and drop a small spoonful into the sauce in between each spiral of salmon. Draw a knife or skewer through the sour cream and into the sauce to make a teardrop shape. Place the reserved tomato pieces on each plate and decorate with watercress leaves.

Facing page: SMOKED SALMON AND SPINACH SPIRALS.

CONSOMMÉ TSARINA

A consommé takes its name from its garnishes, and these are reminiscent of the old Russian Empire of the tsars.

INGREDIENTS

4 cups beef stock □ 1 onion, peeled and chopped □ 1 carrot, finely chopped □ 1 small turnip, peeled and chopped □ 1 small head white cabbage, shredded □ Pinch salt, pepper and sugar □ 1lb raw beet, peeled and finely chopped or grated □ 1 tbsp red wine vinegar □ 2 egg whites □ 2 egg shells, rinsed

GARNISHES

3 hard-boiled eggs □ $^1/_3$ cup mayonnaise □ 3 tbsps stock or water □ 2 tsps gelatin □ $^1/_3$ cup sour cream □ 3 tbsps chopped chives □ Salt and pepper □ Cucumber, cut into small balls or diced □ 2 tomatoes, peeled, seeded and diced □ 2 green onions, thinly sliced □ Caviar or lumpfish roe □ Cooked ham, cut in julienne strips

---

Pour the stock into a large saucepan and add the onion, carrot, turnip and cabbage. Bring to the boil and then allow to simmer for about 30 minutes.

Season lightly with salt and pepper, and add the beet, reserving 3 tbsps for garnishing. Return to the boil and then simmer for a further 10 minutes. Add the vinegar and allow the soup to stand for 20 minutes in the covered saucepan.

Meanwhile, halve the hard-boiled eggs and reserve 1 yolk for garnishing. Chop the remaining eggs finely and combine with the mayonnaise. Soak the gelatin in the stock or water and then dissolve over gentle heat. Pour into the mayonnaise and stir well.

Allow the mixture to cool and then fold in the sour cream, chives and seasoning. Lightly oil 4 small molds and spoon in the mixture. Chill until set. Sieve the reserved egg yolk and prepare the other garnishes.

Strain the soup and discard the vegetables. Pour the soup back into the rinsed out pan. Beat the egg whites lightly and break up the shells. Add both to the soup and bring to the boil slowly, whisking continuously.

Facing page: CONSOMMÉ TSARINA.

Once a thick froth forms on the top of the soup, stop whisking and let the mixture boil up the sides of the pan. Remove from the heat and allow the froth to subside. Repeat twice more without whisking again.

Allow the froth to settle completely and then pour the consommé into a bowl through a colander lined with a clean tea towel. Allow the egg white froth to drop into the colander. Let the consommé drip through the froth and the tea towel slowly. Do not wring out the towel to speed up the process.

Use the ham strips to make a lattice pattern in each soup bowl and place the different garnishes in each space. Unmold the egg mousses and place one in each bowl. Reheat the consommé and carefully spoon it over the garnishes. Serve immediately.

SERVES 4

L EEKS WITH SOUR CREAM

Leeks make an interesting and unusual first course. These look especially attractive arranged on a bed of radicchio with its dark red leaves.

INGREDIENTS

4 medium-sized leeks, well washed □ 1 head radicchio, washed □ 2 tbsps oil □ ½ cup sour cream □ 1 tbsp lemon juice □ Pinch salt, pepper and sugar □ 2 tsps chopped fresh dill

Cut the leeks into even-sized lengths. Tear the radicchio leaves into pieces and use them to line a serving dish.

Heat the oil in a frying pan and add the leeks. Cook slowly to brown slightly and soften. Allow to cool and arrange on the radicchio.

Combine the sour cream, lemon juice, seasoning, sugar and dill and pour the dressing over the leeks to serve.

SERVES 4

Facing page: LEEKS WITH SOUR CREAM.

SOLE AND SPINACH SWIRLS

This fish creation, with its accompaniment of perfectly shaped vegetables, is like a work of art on a plate.

INGREDIENTS
---

4 large sole fillets, skinned □ 8 spinach leaves, blanched □ 2oz cooked ham, chopped □ Dry white wine □ 2 turnips, peeled □ 2 salsify roots, peeled □ 2 small carrots, peeled □ 1 large beet, cooked □ 1 clove garlic, peeled □ 1 cup heavy cream □ 1 stick unsalted butter □ Pinch salt and white pepper □ 1 tbsps lemon juice

---

Cut each fillet into long strips. Wash the spinach leaves well and remove stems and center ribs. Cover the fillet strips with spinach and sprinkle on the chopped ham. Roll up and trim off excess spinach. Place the swirls of fish close together in a baking dish and pour over 1 cup wine.

Cover the baking dish and poach in a preheated 350°F oven for about 15 or 20 minutes. Strain off the liquid and reserve it. Cover the fish and keep it warm.

While the fish is cooking, shape all the vegetables into cylindrical shapes about 2 inches long. Place the turnips and salsify in water, bring to the boil and cook about 3 minutes. Cook the carrots and beet separately for 3 minutes. Keep the vegetables warm.

Bring the reserved fish cooking liquid to the boil in a small saucepan with the garlic. When reduced by half, remove the garlic and discard it.

Pour in the cream and boil rapidly for about 5 minutes. Reduce the heat and whisk in the butter a little at a time. Add seasoning and lemon juice and pour the sauce onto serving plates. Place 2 swirls of sole on each plate and garnish with the vegetables.

SERVES 4

Facing page: SOLE AND SPINACH SWIRLS.

VICHYSSOISE WITH JELLIED VEGETABLES

A cool and creamy potato and leek soup complements a crystal clear mold of jellied vegetables in this elegant appetizer.

──────── INGREDIENTS ────────

4 cups chicken or vegetable stock □ 1 onion, finely diced □ 2 carrots, finely diced □ 2 sticks celery, finely diced □ 3 oz fresh peas □ 1 blade mace □ 1 zucchini, finely diced □ 1 tbsp gelatin □ 4 tbsps dry white wine or water □ 2 tomatoes, peeled, seeded and diced □ 4 tbsps butter or margarine □ 3 leeks, white parts only, well washed □ 1 onion, thinly sliced □ 3 medium potatoes, peeled and thinly sliced □ Salt and white pepper □ 1 bay leaf □ 2 cups milk □ ½ cup heavy cream

──────── GARNISHES ────────

1 lb broccoli flowerets □ 12 asparagus spears □ 2 tomatoes, peeled, seeded and cut into triangles

Bring half of the stock to the boil in a large saucepan. Add the onion, carrots, celery, peas and the blade of mace. Simmer gently for about 20 minutes or until the vegetables are nearly tender. Add the zucchini and cook a further 10 minutes.

Sprinkle the gelatin over the wine or water in a small saucepan. Allow to soak and then dissolve over gentle heat. Remove the blade mace from the stock and vegetables and add the diced tomato. Stir in the gelatin and chill until almost set. Dampen 4 small molds with water and pour in the jellied stock and vegetables. Chill until completely set.

Meanwhile, melt the butter in a large saucepan. Slice the leeks thinly and add to the butter along with the onion and potatoes. Cover and cook very slowly until softened, but not browned. Pour on the remaining stock, season with salt and white pepper and add the bay leaf. Bring to the

Facing page: VICHYSSOISE WITH JELLIED VEGETABLES.

boil and then simmer gently until the vegetables are very soft. Remove the bay leaf, and purée in a food processor or blender, adding some of the milk, if necessary. Add the rest of the milk and chill. When completely cold, stir in the cream.

To prepare the garnishes, bring a pan of water to the boil and blanch the broccoli flowerets and asparagus spears for about 3 minutes. Rinse under cold water and drain. Remore the tips of the asparagus and cut them in half. Slice the stems into thin rounds.

To serve, turn out the jellied vegetable molds into individual soup bowls. Garnish with the blanched vegetables and tomato triangles, and ladle over the vichyssoise.

SERVES 4

RICH DUCK PATE

This pâté is called rillettes in French, and it is the richest pâté you can make. A little goes a long way, but it makes a very luxurious first course.

--- INGREDIENTS ---

5lb duck □ 6oz pork fat □ 6oz pork fillet □ 1 carrot, quartered □ 1 onion, quartered □ 2 bay leaves □ Salt and pepper □ 4 tbsps brandy

Skin the duck and remove the meat. Cut the meat into small pieces and set it aside. Place the duck skin and fat into a deep saucepan. Add the pork fat and cover with water. Cook gently for about 30 minutes. Discard duck bones or keep for stock.

Cut the pork fillet into small pieces and add to the melted fat along with the duck meat. Add the carrot, onion and bay leaves and cover the pan. Cook very slowly for at least 2 hours or until the meat is falling apart. Remove the large pieces of duck skin, carrot, onion and the bay leaves.

Break up the mixture with your hands or a fork, until the meats and fats are well mixed. Adjust the seasoning and add the brandy. Store in the refrigerator. Serve at room temperature with bread or toast.

SERVES 8–10

Facing page: RICH DUCK PÂTÉ.

BORTSCH

This is the famous beet soup made in the traditional way with a good homemade stock as its foundation and a whole complement of vegetables for depth of flavor.

─── INGREDIENTS ───

2 large beef bones □ 4 tbsps rendered beef dripping or oil □ 2 celery stalks, roughly chopped □ 2 carrots, sliced □ 1 small parsnip, sliced □ 1 large onion, sliced □ 1 small head white cabbage □ Bouquet garni (bay leaf, parsley stalk and sprig thyme) □ 10 black peppercorns □ 6 cups water □ 12–14 raw beets □ 2 tbsps red wine vinegar □ Sugar □ Salt □ Sour cream

Above: BORTSCH.

Place the beef bones in a roasting pan and drizzle with dripping or oil. Brown in a hot oven.

Pour the remaining oil into a large stockpot and cook the vegetables, except the beets, until dark brown. Brown slowly so that the vegetables don't burn.

Add the browned bones, bouquet garni, peppercorns and water. Bring to the boil and then simmer, partially covered, for about 2 hours. Skim the surface of the stock as it cooks to remove excess fat. Strain the stock and discard the vegetables and bones.

Meanwhile, scald the beets and peel. Cut 2 into julienne strips and reserve. Chop the rest roughly and combine with the vegetable stock. Cook until tender and purée in several batches in a food processor. Strain, if desired. Add the vinegar, salt and sugar to taste.

To serve, spoon bortsch into soup bowls and top with a swirl of sour cream. Garnish with the reserved julienned beets.

SERVES 8

CHILLED LEEK AND POTATO SOUP

This is a variation on vichyssoise, the famous French soup. Far from being difficult to make, this classic and elegant soup can be easily prepared.

INGREDIENTS
4 leeks, trimmed □ 4 tbsps butter or margarine □ 1 onion, chopped □ 5 medium-sized potatoes, peeled and thinly sliced □ 4 cups water or stock □ Salt, pepper and mace □ 1 bay leaf □ 2 cups milk □ 1 cup sour cream □ Chopped chives to garnish

Use only the white parts of the leeks; slice them thinly. Melt the butter or margarine in a large saucepan and cook the leeks and onion slowly until soft but not colored. Add the potatoes, stock, seasoning, mace and bay leaf.

Cover the pan and bring to the boil. Simmer for about 30 minutes or until the vegetables are soft. Remove the bay leaf. Allow the soup to cool

slightly and then purée in a food processor in 2 or 3 batches until smooth. If desired, push the mixture through a sieve for a smoother texture.

Cool to room temperature and then pour in the milk. Chill in the refrigerator. When completely cold, stir in the sour cream and adjust the seasoning. Sprinkle with chives before serving.

SERVES 6–8

POTATO BLINIS

These are elegant little pancakes made puffy and light with the addition of yeast to their potato batter. For variety, experiment with other toppings.

——————— INGREDIENTS ———————

4oz cooked potatoes ☐ 1 egg ☐ Salt and pepper ☐ 1 tbsp oil ☐ 1 cup all-purpose flour ☐ 1 tsp yeast ☐ 2 cups milk ☐ Oil for frying ☐ 1 smoked trout ☐ 1 small red pepper, seeded and shredded ☐ 1 tbsp white wine vinegar ☐ 3 tbsps oil ☐ Horseradish ☐ 4 green onions, finely chopped

Mix the potatoes, egg, salt, pepper and oil together well. Combine the flour with the yeast in a warm bowl. Heat the milk to a hand-hot temperature and add enough to the flour and yeast to make a thick batter.

Cover the bowl and keep in a warm place for about 1 hour, or until the mixture looks spongy. Reheat the remaining milk slightly and add it to the yeast mixture along with the potato mixture. Cover and leave again for about 1 hour.

When the mixture has risen slightly and looks spongy again, heat a large frying pan and add a small amount of oil. Drop spoonfuls of the batter on to the hot pan and cook on both sides until golden brown. Make the blinis about 3 inches in diameter.

Skin the trout and lift the fillets. Slice the fillets into short, thin slivers and combine with the pepper. Mix the vinegar and oil together well and add a very small amount of horseradish. Combine with the smoked trout and pepper. Spoon the topping into the center of each blini and sprinkle with the chopped onion.

Facing page: POTATO BLINIS.

SHRIMP IN DINNER JACKETS

Shrimp are dressed for dinner in spinach leaf jackets with a garnish of fresh tomato and cucumber. A creamy avocado sauce completes this stylish appetizer.

INGREDIENTS

24 young spinach leaves, stems removed □ 1 cucumber, peeled □ 2 tomatoes, peeled and seeded □ 2 dozen large shrimp, cooked □ 1 large ripe avocado □ 1 tbsp lemon juice □ 1 cup heavy cream □ 1 small clove garlic, crushed □ Salt and white pepper □ Sprigs of fresh herbs (mint, basil or tarragon)

Wash the spinach leaves well and blanch for 1 minute in boiling water. Drain and leave on paper towels to dry completely.

Use a small melonballer to scoop out balls of cucumber. Blanch for 1 minute in boiling water. Rinse under cold water and drain dry.

Cut the tomato flesh into small diamond shapes and set aside to use as a garnish.

Peel the shrimp, leaving on the tips of the tail shells, if desired. Wrap a spinach leaf around each shrimp leaving the ends of the tails exposed.

Cut the avocado in half and remove the stone. Scoop out the pulp, scraping the skin well to remove it all. Purée in a food processor with the lemon juice. Mix the cream by hand and season to taste.

Spoon the sauce onto serving plates and tilt to coat the base of each plate evenly. Place the wrapped shrimp on top of the sauce. Garnish each shrimp with a tomato diamond and place cucumber balls on each plate. Add the fresh herbs and serve immediately.

SERVES 4

Facing page: SHRIMP IN DINNER JACKETS.

Chapter 2
DELICATE DISHES

Surprise Packages

Little packages of vegetable leaves contain seafood surprises in this beautifully presented dinner party appetizer. Other varieties of seafood can make interesting fillings, too.

INGREDIENTS

2 leeks, well washed □ 6 spinach leaves, well washed □ 6 green cabbage leaves □ 6 oysters □ 6 scallops □ 6 slices smoked salmon □ 1 shallot, chopped □ 1 bay leaf □ ½ cup dry white wine □ 1 cup fish or vegetable stock □ Pinch saffron □ 1 cup heavy cream □ Salt and white pepper □ Fresh chives

Cut along the length of the leeks, but not completely in half. Separate the layers and wash them well. Cut off the green parts and save the white parts for another use. Blanch the green parts in boiling water for 3–4 minutes or until pliable. Rinse under cold water and leave to drain.

Remove the stems and center rib from the spinach leaves and blanch them for 30 seconds. Drain well.

Trim down the thick ribs in the cabbage leaves and blanch the leaves for about 1–2 minutes or until just pliable. Rinse under cold water.

Wrap each oyster in a spinach leaf. Wrap each scallop in a cabbage leaf. Fold up the smoked salmon slices into a 2 inch square and wrap in 1 layer of leek. Wrap around another layer of leek in the opposite direction from the first. Place the packages on a rack and steam for about 8 minutes.

To prepare the sauce, place the shallot and bay leaf in a medium saucepan and pour in the wine and stock. Add the saffron and bring to the boil. Cook rapidly to reduce by two-thirds.

Strain the mixture into a clean saucepan and add the cream. Bring back to the boil and cook rapidly for 5 minutes to thicken the cream. Taste and add salt and white pepper.

Chop about 1 tbsp of the chives, leaving some whole for garnishing. Spoon the sauce onto serving plates and place one oyster, 1 scallop and 1 smoked salmon package on each plate. Scatter whole chives over each serving as a garnish.

Previous page: Chicken Pilaff.
Facing page: Surprise Packages.

SHELLFISH FANTASIA

Deserving of its name, this recipe is a fantasy of shellfish and vegetables. It is complicated, but worth every second spent on preparation.

INGREDIENTS

4 cups fish or vegetable stock ☐ 2 cups dry white wine ☐ 1 tbsp gelatin ☐ 1 bay leaf ☐ 1 sprig fresh rosemary ☐ 1 clove garlic, peeled and left whole ☐ Peel of 1 lemon, pith removed ☐ 1lb mussels ☐ 2 live lobsters ☐ 1 leek, well washed and thinly sliced ☐ 1 carrot, thinly sliced ☐ 1 green onion, sliced ☐ 4oz broccoli ☐ ½ small cauliflower ☐ 8 asparagus spears ☐ 2 tomatoes, peeled, seeded and diced ☐ Fresh coriander ☐ 2oz pea pods, topped and tailed ☐ 4 tiny zucchini, topped and tailed

Pour the stock into a large saucepan with a tight-fitting lid. Pour 4 tbsps of the wine into a small saucepan and sprinkle over the gelatin. Set it aside to soak and add the rest of the wine to the stock. Add the bay leaf, rosemary, garlic and lemon peel to the stock and wine and bring to the boil.

Meanwhile, scrub the mussel shells well and remove the seaweed beards. Discard any mussels with broken shells or those that do not close when tapped.

Once the stock mixture comes to the boil, remove it from the heat and allow it to cool slightly. Place in the live lobsters and bring gently back to the boil. Cook about 10 minutes and add the mussels. Cook a further 2–3 minutes, or until the mussel shells open.

Remove the shellfish and discard any mussels that have not opened. Strain the cooking liquid through a fine sieve and return it to the rinsed out pan.

Add the leek and carrot to the liquid and bring back to the boil. Cook about 3 minutes and add the green onion. Cut the broccoli and cauliflower into small flowerets and add to the pan. Cut the tips off the asparagus and slice in half. Cut the stems into small dice. Add to the pan and cook all the vegetables for a further 3 minutes. Remove all the vegetables and set them aside.

Facing page: SHELLFISH FANTASIA.

Remove the mussels from their shells, reserving a few for garnishing, if desired. Crack the lobsters and remove the meat. Leave the claw meat whole, if possible, and cut the tail meat in half. Set the shellfish aside with the vegetables.

Dissolve the gelatin and wine over gentle heat. Remove about $1/3$ of the cooking liquid from the pan and combine it with the gelatin. Chill until syrupy.

Dampen 4 small molds with water and pour in a small amount of the mixture. Chill until set. Arrange some of the cooked vegetables and shellfish in layers, setting each layer with more jellied mixture. Chill until completely set.

Blanch the pea pods in boiling water for 1 minute and remove. Cook the zucchini for about 3 minutes, or until just tender. Slice thinly, lengthwise.

To serve, unmold the jellied mixtures into serving bowls. Garnish with pea pods, zucchini and one of the tomatoes. Reheat the soup and add the shellfish and remaining tomato. Spoon the hot soup around the jellies and garnish with coriander leaves. Serve immediately.

SERVES 4

MOUSSE D'AVOCAT AUX MOULES

A savory mousse is always impressive as a first course, and this one made with avocado and mussels is an unusual one as well. A creamy basil sauce sets it all off.

INGREDIENTS

2 large ripe avocados □ 1 cup cream cheese □ 2 eggs □ 4 tbsps lemon juice □ 1 tbsp gelatin □ Salt and pepper □ 8oz shelled cooked mussels □ Oil □ 4 tbsps dry white wine □ $1/3$ cup stock □ 1 cup heavy cream □ 1 tbsp chopped fresh basil □ 1 carrot, peeled and thinly sliced □ 1 zucchini, thinly sliced

Facing page: MOUSSE D'AVOCAT AUX MOULES.

Cut the avocados in half and remove the stones. Scrape out the pulp into a food processor. Add the cream cheese and eggs and purée until smooth. Soak the gelatin in the lemon juice and then dissolve over gentle heat. Pour into the avocado mixture with the machine running. Season with salt and pepper.

Lightly oil 6 small molds and place 4 mussels in the bottom of each one. Spoon over the avocado mixture and chill until set.

Meanwhile combine the wine and stock in a small saucepan and bring to the boil. Cook rapidly to reduce by half. Add the cream, and boil 2–3 minutes to thicken. Season with salt and pepper and stir in the basil. Leave to cool.

Blanch the carrot slices and zucchini slices in separate pans. Drain and rinse under cold water. Pat dry.

To serve, unmold the avocado mousses onto serving plates and spoon the basil cream sauce over each one. Garnish the plates with the carrot and zucchini slices and remaining mussels.

SERVES 6

GREEN VEGETABLE FLANS

Tender pastry forms cases for fresh green vegetables in a creamy custard. These are good for appetizers or light meals anytime. Serve them hot or cold.

─────────── INGREDIENTS ───────────

1½ cups all purpose flour ☐ Pinch salt ☐ ⅓ cup butter or margarine
☐ Cold water

─────────── FILLING ───────────

6oz green vegetables (such as zucchini, broccoli, asparagus, green beans or leeks) ☐ 2 eggs and 3 egg yolks ☐ 1 cup heavy cream ☐ ½ cup finely grated sharp cheese ☐ Salt and pepper ☐ Pinch nutmeg and cayenne pepper ☐ Chopped chives

Facing page: GREEN VEGETABLE FLANS.

Sift the flour with a pinch of salt into a large bowl. Rub in the butter or margarine until the mixture resembles fine breadcrumbs. Mix in enough cold water to make a firm dough. Chill for 20 minutes.

Cook the vegetables in boiling salted water until just barely tender. Drain well. Mix the whole eggs and egg yolks with the cream and cheese and add salt, pepper, nutmeg and cayenne.

Roll out the pastry and line 6 4 × 3 inch tart pans. Trim the edges and fill with the vegetables. Spoon over the custard and sprinkle with chives.

Preheat a metal baking tray in a 350°F oven and place the tart pans on it. Bake for about 25 minutes or until the custard is set and the pastry is golden brown. A knife inserted into the center of each flan should come out clean.

SERVES 6

*L*OBSTER TERRINE WITH MUSHROOM CREAMS

When an ingredient is as expensive and luxurious as lobster, the recipe must do it justice.
This one is extremely elegant.

─────────── INGREDIENTS ───────────

1 large lobster, cooked □ 4 tbsps butter □ 8oz mushrooms, thinly sliced □ 6 eggs, beaten □ 6 tbsps cream cheese □ 1½ cups heavy cream □ Salt and pepper □ 1 tbsp gelatin □ 1 cup white wine □ 1 shallot, finely chopped □ 1 egg yolk □ Extra mushrooms and dill for garnishing

Break off the large claws and small legs of the lobster. Reserve the small legs for garnishing. Crack the lobster and large claws and extract the meat. Slice the tail meat and claw meat thinly.

Facing page: LOBSTER TERRINE WITH MUSHROOM CREAMS.

Melt the butter and cook the mushrooms for a few minutes. Combine ¼ of the mushrooms with the eggs. Beat the cream cheese until soft, and gradually add ½ cup of the cream. Combine with the eggs and mushrooms and season with salt and pepper.

Add the lobster body meat and pour the mixture into a lightly oiled loaf pan lined with wax paper. Place the sliced lobster on top and cover the pan with foil. Set the loaf pan in a roasting pan of hot water to come halfway up the sides. Cook in a preheated 325 F oven until a skewer inserted into the middle comes out clean. Leave to cool at room temperature and then refrigerate.

Sprinkle the gelatin on top of the wine and leave to soak. Dissolve over gentle heat. Add the shallot to the remaining mushrooms and continue to cook until the vegetables are soft.. Purée in a food processor along with the egg yolk. Add the gelatin and wine through the funnel with the machine running.

Whip the remaining cream lightly and fold into the mixture by hand. Pour the mixture in 6 small molds that have been lightly oiled. Chill until set.

To serve, turn out the mushroom creams onto serving plates. Turn out the lobster terrine and slice into equal portions. Garnish the plate with the reserved lobster legs and the mushroom creams with extra mushrooms and dill.

SERVES 6

CHICKEN PILAFF

This chicken and rice dish gets its attractive look and unusual taste from the use of edible flowers like marigolds, violets and roses.

───────────── INGREDIENTS ─────────────

3lbs chicken, skinned and boned □ Oil for frying □ 8oz long-grain rice □ 1 onion, thinly sliced □ ¼ cup pinenuts □ ¼ cup pistachio nuts □ ¼ tsp cinnamon □ ¼ tsp coriander □ 1½ cups chicken stock □ ½ cup dried apricots, chopped □ 2 green onions, chopped □ Salt and pepper □ Fresh marigold, violet and rose petals, well washed

Cut the chicken into thin strips. Heat oil in a large sauté pan and cook the chicken quickly until lightly browned. Remove and set aside.

Above: CHICKEN PILAFF.

Cook the rice and sliced onion until the onion is lightly browned. Add the pinenuts and pistachios and fry briefly. Add the cinnamon and coriander and pour on the stock.

Cover the pan and cook slowly until the stock evaporates by half and the rice is nearly tender. Return the chicken to the pan and add the apricots and green onions. Cover again and cook until the rice is completely tender and the stock evaporated.

Adjust the seasoning and sprinkle with flower petals to serve.

SERVES 4–6

PASTRY AND PATE LAYERS

Two contrasts of texture, silky smooth pâté and crisp flan pastry, combine beautifully in a first course that is as delicious as it looks.

INGREDIENTS
---

1 cup flour ☐ Pinch salt ☐ 1 tbsp sugar ☐ 4 tbsps butter, softened ☐ 1 egg yolk ☐ 4 tbsps water ☐ 1¼lbs chicken liver pâté ☐ ⅓ cup unsalted butter, creamed ☐ 4 tbsps ground almonds ☐ 3 tbsps dry sherry ☐ 10 black olives, pitted and sliced, or 1 sliced truffle ☐ 2 cups prepared aspic (optional) ☐ Small bunches of grapes (optional)

Sift the flour and salt onto a clean work surface. Make a well in the center and place the sugar, butter, egg yolk and water in the well.

Cream the sugar, butter, egg yolk and water together until the mixture looks like scrambled eggs. Toss the flour over the mixture and work it in gradually until a smooth paste forms. Wrap and chill for 1 hour.

Combine the chicken liver pâté, unsalted butter, almonds and sherry until smooth.

Roll out the pastry on a floured surface to a rectangle about ¼ inch thick. Cut into 4 long rectangles. Place on baking sheets and bake in a preheated 400°F oven until pale golden brown. Do not allow the pastry to get too dark. Allow to cool a few minutes on the baking sheets and then remove the pastry to wire racks to cool.

When completely cold, sandwich the layers together with the pâté mixture, adding the olives to the middle layer and ending with pastry on top. Chill until firm. To serve, cut with a serrated knife. If desired, flood plates with aspic and set a decoration of grapes on each. Chill until set, and place pastry and pâté layers on top.

SERVES 8

Facing page: Pastry and Pâte Layers.

CHEDDAR PEARS WITH WATERCRESS CREAM

The traditional plump shape of William or Comice pears makes them ideal for serving whole. Savory uses for pears are unusual, and this one is especially attractive.

INGREDIENTS

6 ripe William or Comice pears □ Lemon juice □ 6 tbsps soft cheese (curd, cream or low fat) □ ¾ cup mature Cheddar cheese, finely grated □ Pinch nutmeg and cayenne pepper □ 2 cups heavy cream □ Pinch salt, white pepper and sugar □ 1 bunch watercress, washed □ 1 small head iceberg lettuce, washed and finely shredded

Core the pears, but leave the stems attached. Peel the pears and brush them inside and out with lemon juice to prevent discoloration.

Mix the soft cheese, Cheddar, nutmeg and cayenne together to a smooth paste. If too thick, add a spoonful of heavy cream. Fill a pastry bag fitted with a plain tube with the cheese mixture and pipe into the hollows in each pear. Place the pears on serving plates.

Whip ½ cup of the cream very lightly to thicken slightly. Add 1 tsp lemon juice and a pinch of sugar. Spoon this mixture over each pear.

Remove the thick stems and roots from the watercress and reserve some of the smaller leaves to garnish the plates. Chop the rest in a food processor.

Bring the remaining cream to a rapid boil and allow to reduce by about ¹/₃. Add the chopped watercress and cook slowly for 2 minutes. Purée the mixture in a food processor until smooth. Allow to cool to room temperature and spoon around the pears.

Arrange shreds of lettuce around the base of each pear and serve.

SERVES 6

Facing page: CHEDDAR PEARS WITH WATERCRESS CREAM.

Chapter 3

FISH AND SEAFOOD

SPECIAL STEAMED SHRIMP

A dish made with large shrimp just has to be special. Though this looks impressive and complicated it's very easy to achieve.

INGREDIENTS

12 raw large shrimp, unpeeled □ 4 tbsps white or rice wine □ Sesame seed oil □ 1 lemon □ 1 turnip, peeled □ ½ red pepper, seeded and finely shredded □ ½ green pepper, seeded and finely shredded

Remove the legs from the shrimp. Cut down the length of the rounded side of the tails, press open and flatten.

Above: SPECIAL STEAMED SHRIMP.

Sprinkle with the wine and sesame seed oil. Pare off the lemon peel and scrape to remove all the white pith. Cut the peel in very fine shreds.

Slice the turnip thinly and cut the slices into very fine shreds. Garnish the shrimp with the lemon peel and vegetables. Squeeze a few drops of the lemon juice over each shrimp. Place on a rack above simmering water and steam for about 10 minutes. Serve immediately.

SERVES 6 AS A FIRST COURSE

SHRIMP AND EGG PILAFF

A rice pilaff with extra ingredients such as shrimp and eggs makes a delicious light meal, and only needs a salad or vegetable to complete it.

--- INGREDIENTS ---

1 cup long grain rice □ 4 tbsps butter or margarine □ 1 onion, thinly sliced □ 1 tsp ground ginger □ 2 cups chicken or vegetable stock □ Few strands saffron □ 1 bay leaf □ Salt and pepper □ 4oz cooked, peeled shrimp □ 3 hard-boiled eggs, chopped

Rinse the rice well to remove the starch and leave it to drain.

Melt the butter or margarine in a large saucepan and cook the onion slowly until golden brown. Add the rice and cook until the grains turn opaque.

Pour on the stock and add the saffron and bay leaf. Bring to the boil, cover and simmer until the rice is tender and has absorbed most of the stock. If the rice cooks before most of the stock has been absorbed, remove the pan lid and boil rapidly.

Season to taste with salt and pepper and remove the bay leaf. Stir in the shrimp and eggs, cover and press the mixture into well-buttered oven-proof 2 pint bowl or mold. Place in a moderate oven for about 15 minutes to heat through. Turn out onto a serving dish.

SERVES 8

FEUILLTEES DE POISSON FUME

A combination of buttery pastry and smoked fish makes a lovely first course. It's so good, you might want to make a whole meal of it!

————————— INGREDIENTS —————————

1lb puff pastry □ 1 egg, beaten with a pinch of salt □ 2 tbsps butter □ 1lb tomatoes, peeled, seeded and chopped □ 4 tbsps dry vermouth □ ½ tsp chopped dill □ Pinch salt, pepper and sugar □ 4oz smoked salmon □ 1 large smoked trout □ 4 tsps heavy cream □ 1 tbsp prepared horseradish □ Lumpfish caviar and sprigs of dill for garnishing

Draw a fish shape on paper and cut out a pattern. Roll out the pastry to a thickness of ½ inch and cut out 6 fish. Brush the tops with the beaten egg glaze and mark with a sharp knife to form 'scales', if desired.

Place the pastry fish on a lightly oiled baking sheet sprinkled with water. Bake in a preheated 400°F oven until the pastry is golden brown and risen.

Meanwhile melt the butter in a medium saucepan and add the tomatoes, vermouth and dill. Cook until the tomatoes soften completely. Purée in a food processor and add salt, pepper and sugar to taste.

Cut the smoked salmon into small strips. Skin and bone the smoked trout and cut the fillets into slivers. Mix the cream and the horseradish and combine with the smoked fish.

Allow the pastry to cool slightly and cut in half. Place the bottom half of each fish on a serving plate. Spoon on the smoked fish filling and place on the pastry tops. Decorate with the caviar and sprigs of dill and spoon the sauce around each fish.

SERVES 6

Facing page: FEUILLTÉES DE POISSON FUMÉ.

SEVICHE OF SARDINES

The sardines in this recipe 'cook' in their marinade in the refrigerator. For this dish, the fish must be absolutely fresh.

───────────── INGREDIENTS ─────────────

1½lbs fresh sardines, filleted □ 6 limes □ 2 tbsps oil □ Pinch salt and pepper □ 2 tbsps prepared horseradish □ ½ cup sour cream □ 6oz cooked green beans □ Flat parsley leaves □ Red lumpfish caviar

Place the sardines in a shallow dish. Mix the juice of 4 limes with the oil, seasoning and horseradish. Pour over the fish and turn to coat evenly. Cover the dish and refrigerate for at least 4 hours.

Remove the fish from the marinade and place on a serving dish. Mix the sour cream into the marinade and spoon over the fish. Garnish the dish with the beans, parsley and caviar.

SERVES 4

SEA FLOWERS

This is one of the prettiest fish dishes ever. Specialist greengrocers or gardening friends can provide the zucchini blossoms.

───────────── INGREDIENTS ─────────────

4 fillets of halibut or turbot □ 1 small carrot, sliced □ ½ stick celery, sliced □ ½ small onion, sliced □ 1 bouquet garni (bay leaf, sprig thyme, parsley stalks) □ 4 zucchini □ 8 zucchini blossoms □ 1/3 cup white wine □ 1 tsp coriander seeds □ 2 tbsps orange juice □ 1 stick unsalted butter

Facing page: SEVICHE OF SARDINES.

Skin the fish fillets and place the skins in a saucepan with the carrot, celery and onion. Add the bouquet garni and pour on 1½ cups water. Bring slowly to the boil and then simmer for 15 minutes. Strain and reserve the stock.

Cut 1 zucchini into very thin petal-like strips. Blanch the strips for 30 seconds in boiling water and drain on paper towels. Chop the remaining zucchini finely and sprinkle with salt and pepper. Wash the zucchini blossoms, open out and stuff with the chopped zucchinis.

Place the stuffed zucchini blossoms on a steamer rack and set above simmering water. Cover tightly and steam for 6 minutes.

Cut the fillets into thin slices and place in a frying pan. Pour over the reserved stock, cover and poach gently for 10–15 minutes or until just firm. Keep the fish warm and strain 1 cup of the stock into a saucepan.

Add the wine and coriander seed to the stock and boil very rapidly to reduce by half. Add the orange juice and begin beating the butter into the sauce bit by bit. Do not allow the sauce to boil when adding the butter.

Strain the sauce onto serving plates and arrange the fish 'petals' on the sauce. Place the zucchini 'petals' on top of the fish and add 2 stuffed zucchini blossoms to each serving.

SERVES 4

SEA BASS ASPERGE

Sea bass is a good choice of fish for an elegant dish like this. Asparagus complements the taste without distracting from it.

INGREDIENTS

4 fillets of sea bass, about 8oz each □ 2 onion slices □ 2 cups dry white wine □ 2 star anise □ 1¾lb white asparagus □ ½ cup heavy cream □ Salt and pepper □ 8 pieces star anise □ Small bunch chives □ Small bunch tarragon leaves □ Coriander leaves

Place the fish in a saute pan with the onion, wine and 2 star anise. Cover and bring to simmering. Cook for 1 minute and remove the fish to a low oven to keep warm. Cover well with foil. Reserve the cooking liquid.

Previous page: SEA FLOWERS.

Trim the asparagus stalks and cook in a steamer until just tender.

Strain the fish cooking liquid into a saucepan and bring to a rapid boil to reduce by half. Add the cream and boil to thicken. Season with salt and pepper.

Arrange a fillet of bass on each plate and place asparagus next to it. Spoon the sauce over each fillet. Make a flower with the star anise, chives and tarragon on each piece of fish and garnish with a coriander sprig.

SERVES 4

Above: SEA BASS ASPERGE.

TURBANS OF SALMON

This smoked salmon mousse is quickly made but looks far more complicated. Powdered aspic is easy to use and, when mixed with water, sets to give the salmon a shiny glaze.

───────────────── INGREDIENTS ─────────────────

¾ cup prepared aspic □ 8oz smoked salmon □ 3 tbsps dry white wine □ ½ tbsp gelatin □ ½ cup mayonnaise □ ½ cup whipping cream □ Pinch salt and white pepper □ Lemon wedges for garnishing

Make up the aspic from a packet using boiling water. Allow it to cool until syrupy.

Cut the best slices of the smoked salmon to fit the bases and sides of 4 small molds with a ¾ cup capacity.

Above: TURBANS OF SALMON.

Dampen the molds with water. Dip the cut pieces of salmon in the aspic and use to line the molds. Chill until set.

Sprinkle the gelatin on the wine in a small saucepan. Leave to soak about 5 minutes then dissolve over low heat.

Combine the remaining aspic with the remaining salmon, mayonnaise, salt and pepper in a food processor. Purée until smooth and then mix in the gelatin.

Whip the cream and fold in by hand. Spoon the mixture into the salmon-lined molds and smooth the top. Fold over any overlapping ends of the salmon.

Chill the molds until set. To unmold, loosen from the sides and invert onto a plate. Shake sharply to release the salmon. Garnish with lemon wedges to serve.

SERVES 4

COQUILLES ST JACQUES A LA CREME

Cook scallops for the shortest time possible to make sure they are served at their tender best. A rich cream sauce dotted with shallots is perfect for them.

--- INGREDIENTS ---

12 or 24 small large scallops with roes □ ½ cup dry white wine □ 1 shallot, finely chopped □ 1 bay leaf □ 1 sprig thyme □ 1 blade mace □ 1 cup cream □ Pinch salt and white pepper

If using large scallops, cut them horizontally in half or in thirds, leaving the roes whole. Place them in a saucepan and add the wine, shallot, bay leaf, thyme and mace. Poach over very gentle heat for 3–5 minutes. Remove them and keep them warm.

Remove the bay leaf, thyme and mace from the wine and add the cream. Bring to the boil and cook for about 3 minutes to thicken. Season with salt and pepper to taste. Pour over the scallops to serve. Accompany the dish with cooked white, brown or wild rice.

SERVES 4

LETTUCE AND LANGOUSTINE PARCELS

Surprise packages are always exciting and these are no exception. Other shellfish can be used instead of the langoustines with equally delicious results.

INGREDIENTS

2 heads round or 1 leaf lettuce □ 2 tbsps butter □ 12 langoustines □ 3 green onions, finely chopped □ 1 inch piece fresh ginger, finely chopped □ 1 red pepper, seeded and chopped □ 4oz mushrooms, finely chopped □ Salt and pepper □ 2 cups dry white wine □ 1 cup fish stock □ 1 tbsp chopped chives □ 1 tbsp chopped parsley □ 1 stick unsalted butter □ Small bunch coriander □ Small bunch chives □ 3½oz jar red lumpfish caviar □ Capers or green peppercorns

Above: LETTUCE AND LANGOUSTINE PARCELS.

Separate the lettuce leaves and wash well. Blanch in boiling water for 30 seconds, drain and rinse under cold water.

Melt the butter in a saucepan and cook the langoustines, onions, ginger and red pepper for 3 minutes. Reserve 6 even-sized mushrooms and trim off the stems. Chop the stems and the rest of the mushrooms finely and add to the shellfish and vegetables. Cook a further 2 minutes and adjust the seasoning. Divide and wrap the mixture in 12 of the largest lettuce leaves.

Bring the wine and stock to the boil and cook rapidly to reduce by half. Add the lettuce parcels and heat through. Remove them to hot serving plates.

Add the butter a piece at a time to the liquid, whisking well until the sauce thickens. Stir in the chopped chives and parsley. Pour around the parcels. Garnish the plate with coriander leaves, whole chives, red caviar and a mushroom. Place a caper or peppercorn on each mushroom and serve immediately.

SERVES 6

SMOKED SALMON AND HALIBUT SLICES ON LIME CREAM

A beautifully arranged first course sets the tone for the rest of the meal. Smoked salmon is always popular, and smoked halibut is a tasty surprise.

—————————— INGREDIENTS ——————————

4oz smoked salmon, thinly sliced □ 4oz smoked halibut, thinly sliced □ ½ cup sour cream □ ½ cup heavy cream, lightly whipped □ Juice and grated rind of 1 lime □ Salt and pepper □ Pinch ground ginger □ 1 tsp chopped fresh dill □ Dill and basil to garnish □ Cherry tomatoes and lime slices to garnish □ Pink peppercorns

Layer up slices of salmon and halibut and roll up. Cut into thin slices and place cut side down on a chopping board. Flatten slightly.

Mix the sour cream and whipped cream with the lime juice and rind. Add salt, pepper and a pinch of ginger. Stir in the chopped dill and spread the sauce onto 4 plates.

Arrange the slices of fish on top and garnish with dill and basil. Cut cherry tomatoes into diamonds and add to the plate along with lime slices. Sprinkle on pink peppercorns and serve.

SERVES 4

EMBROIDERED FISH

The colorful garnish of brown, white, green, red and orange provides the embroidery for this fish dressed up in its dinner party best.

--- INGREDIENTS ---

4 dried Chinese mushrooms, soaked in hot water □ 4 green onions □ 1 large red pepper, seeded and shredded □ 1 large carrot, peeled and finely grated □ 1 snapper or bream, weighing about 2lbs, cleaned □ 2 cloves garlic, crushed □ 2 inch piece fresh ginger, peeled and sliced □ Soy sauce □ Canned gingko nuts or water chestnuts (optional) □ Spinach leaves, well washed □ 1 lemon, thinly sliced

Leave the mushrooms in water for about 30 minutes to soften. Remove stalks and slice the caps finely.

Separate the white and green parts of the onions. Shred each finely and keep separate. Prepare the other vegetables and set them aside.

Make five or six cuts on the best-looking side of the fish. Place the garlic and ginger in the fish cavity and sprinkle inside with soy sauce.

Stuff each of the cuts with the prepared vegetables. Place the fish on the rack of a steamer and set over simmering water. Cover tightly and steam until the fish is tender. About 5 minutes before the fish is ready, add the gingko nuts or water chestnuts to the steamer to cook alongside the fish.

To serve, line a serving plate with spinach leaves and carefully place the fish on top. Garnish with lemon slices and the gingko nuts or water chestnuts. Serve with steamed or fried rice.

Above: EMBROIDERED FISH.

SHRIMP IN COGNAC

This must be the fastest first course on earth! Because of its simplicity, the flavor of the shrimp is all important, so they must be fresh.

INGREDIENTS

3lbs cooked, unpeeled shrimp □ 3 tbsps unsalted butter □ Freshly ground
black pepper □ ⅓ cup cognac

Remove all the small legs from the shrimp. Melt the butter in a large frying pan and add the shrimp.

Toss over high heat for a few minutes. Heat the cognac in a small pan and ignite with a match. Pour it over the shrimp while flaming and shake the frying pan until the flames disappear. Serve immediately.

SERVES 4

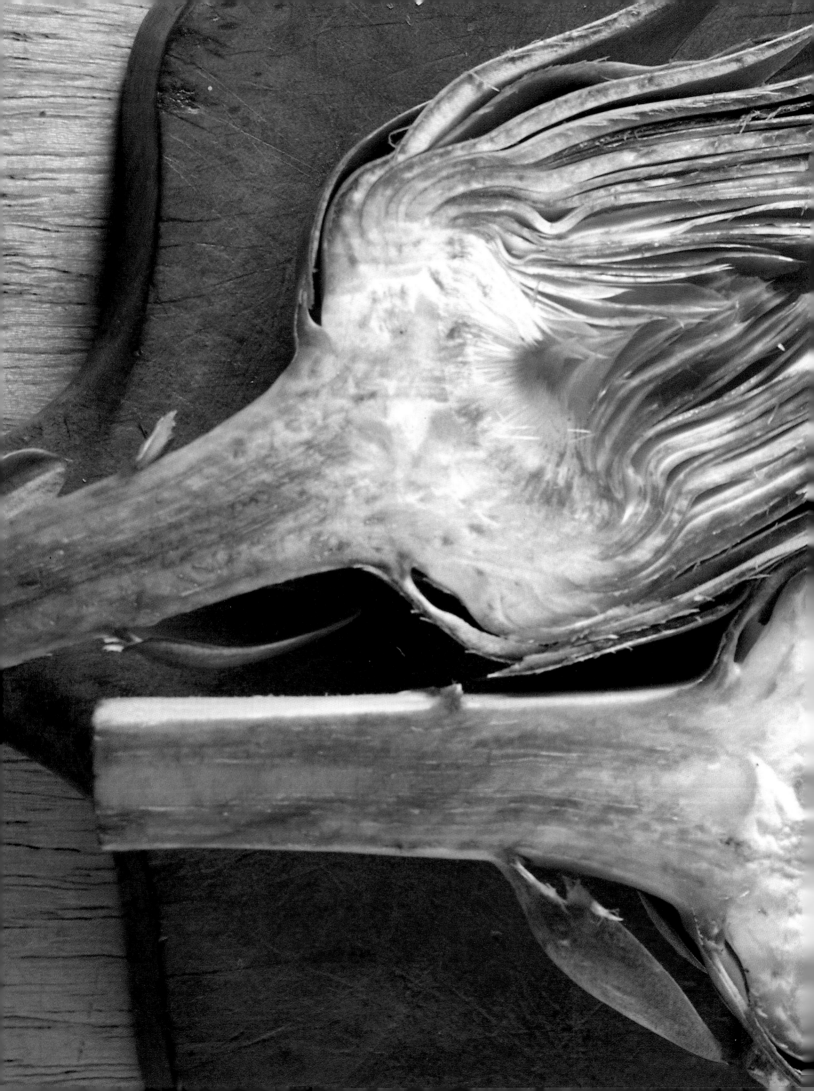

Chapter 4

SALAD DISHES

PALM ISLAND SALAD

Hearts of palm are an unusual ingredient, but are usually found in cans on any supermarket shelf. They provide a good contrast to the velvety texture of avocado.

―――――――――――― INGREDIENTS ――――――――――――

Juice of 2 limes ☐ ¹/₃ cup olive oil ☐ Pinch sugar ☐ Salt and pepper ☐ 2 avocados ☐ 15oz canned hearts of palm, drained and rinsed ☐ 2oz piece fresh Parmesan cheese

―――

Combine the lime juice, olive oil, sugar, salt and pepper and blend very well. Cut the avocados in half and remove the stones. Peel and slice the avocados thinly. Place in the dressing immediately.

Cut the hearts of palm in ½ inch-thick strips and toss with the avocados. Do not allow the avocado slices to break up. Use a vegetable peeler or cheese slicer to pare off thin strips of Parmesan cheese to scatter over the top of the salad.

FENNEL, ORANGE AND WATERCRESS

A refreshing salad that couldn't be easier to prepare, this makes a quick and colorful appetizer or a nice accompaniment to grilled meat, poultry or fish.

―――――――――――― INGREDIENTS ――――――――――――

1 head fennel ☐ 2 tbsps lemon juice ☐ 3 oranges ☐ 1 bunch watercress ☐ Grapeseed oil ☐ Pinch sugar and mustard powder ☐ Salt and pepper

―――

Core the fennel and slice it thinly. Place in a bowl with the lemon juice and toss to coat.

―――――――――――――――――――――――――――――――――――

Facing page: PALM ISLAND SALAD.

Peel and segment the oranges over a bowl to collect the juice. Add the segments to the fennel. Pick over the watercress and discard the roots and thick stalks. Add the watercress to the fennel and oranges.

Measure the orange juice and add 3 tbsps oil for every 1 tbsp juice. Whisk in the sugar, mustard, salt and pepper. Pour over the salad and toss to serve.

SALADE JULIENNE

Strips of vegetables, crunchy walnuts, curls of orange peel and delicately flavored lamb's lettuce make up this perfectly arranged salad that makes a very impressive first course.

INGREDIENTS

4 small beets ☐ 4 sticks celery ☐ 1 celeriac root, peeled ☐ Juice of 1 lemon ☐ 1 orange ☐ 32 walnut halves ☐ 8 small bunches lamb's lettuce (mache) ☐ ½ cup light cream ☐ ½ cup white Stilton ☐ ½ tsp horseradish cream ☐ Salt and pepper

Above: SALADE JULIENNE.

Peel the beets and cut into thin strips. Cut the celery and celeriac in strips of similar size. Toss the celeriac strips in lemon juice to prevent discoloration.

Pare the rind off the orange in thin strips and blanch in boiling water for 1 minute. Drain and rinse under cold water. Arrange the vegetables on serving plates and top the beet strips with orange rind. Arrange walnut halves next to the vegetables and lamb's lettuce in the middle.

Squeeze the juice from the orange and combine with any remaining lemon juice. Process with the remaining ingredients in a food processor until smooth. Serve the dressing separately.

SERVES 4

Salade au Fromage

Almost any variety of cheese tastes wonderful in this salad, so choose your favorite. It's a recipe that's both easy and colorful.

INGREDIENTS

1 head lettuce, washed □ 1 small cucumber, sliced □ 4–6 tomatoes, depending on size, thinly sliced □ 8oz cheese, diced □ 1 red pepper, diced □ 1 green pepper, diced □ 4 tsps chopped parsley □ 8 black olives, pitted

LEMON DRESSING

3 tbsps lemon juice □ ½ cup vegetable oil □ 1 green onion, very finely chopped □ Salt and pepper □ Pinch sugar (optional)

Break the lettuce into separate leaves and arrange on salad plates.

Overlap the cucumber and tomato slices in a circle, alternating the two ingredients.

Place piles of diced cheese and peppers in the center of the circle and sprinkle on chopped parsley.

Slice the black olives and arrange on top of the cucumber and tomato slices.

Mix the dressing ingredients together in a food processor until well emulsified and creamy looking. Spoon over the salad to serve.

SERVES 4

GAMMON ON ENDIVE DRESSED WITH ROSEMARY

Warm salads such as this one make unusual first courses or light main dishes. Its many parts can be prepared in advance and then assembled later.

──────────── INGREDIENTS ────────────

1½lb joint country ham, soaked overnight □ Brown sugar □ Oil □ 2 bread rolls, sliced thinly □ 1 head curly endive □ Small head oakleaf lettuce □ ½ cup walnut and vegetable oil, mixed □ 3 tbsps white wine vinegar □ 3 sprigs fresh rosemary, leaves only □ Salt and pepper □ ½ tsp mild mustard

Score the outside fat of the ham and sprinkle with sugar. Roast in a preheated 375°F oven for about 1–1½ hours. Allow to cool.

Heat about 1 inch of oil in a large frying pan. When hot, put in the slices of rolls. Cook until golden and crisp. Remove to paper towels to drain.

Wash and dry the lettuces well and break into separate leaves. Heat the salad oils slightly and mix in the vinegar, rosemary leaves, seasoning and mustard. Slice the ham thinly and arrange on beds of lettuce. Garnish with the crôuton slices and spoon over the warm dressing. Serve immediately.

Facing page: SALADE AU FROMAGE.
Overleaf: GAMMON ON ENDIVE DRESSED WITH ROSEMARY.

Spiced Wheat and Walnut Salad

Bulgur wheat has a slightly nutty flavor that goes very well with herbs and spices. This easy-to-prepare salad makes a good appetizer for an informal dinner party.

—————————— INGREDIENTS ——————————

¾ cup bulgur wheat □ 1 small onion, peeled and grated □ 1 tsp chili powder □ ¼ tsp cinnamon □ 2 tsps chopped fresh oregano □ 2 tbsps chopped parsley □ ¾ cup chopped walnuts □ 1 tbsp tomato paste □ 4 tbsps olive oil □ 1 tbsp white wine vinegar □ Salt and pepper
□ Cayenne pepper (optional)

Soak the bulgur wheat in cold water to cover, until the grains expand and absorb most of the water. Drain and spread out on a clean towel to dry. Fluff up the grains occasionally to keep separate.

Combine the remaining ingredients in a large bowl, add the bulgur wheat and toss well. Add cayenne pepper for extra hotness, if desired. Refrigerate for at least several hours for the flavors to blend. The salad can be prepared a day in advance.

SERVES 4–6

Salade Melange

An array of colorful vegetables makes up this fresh salad. The choice of vegetables can be altered to suit the season and individual tastes.

—————————— INGREDIENTS ——————————

4oz each of the following vegetables: □ Asparagus □ Green beans □ Peas □ Sweetcorn □ Carrots □ Potatoes □ Turnips

Facing page: SALADE MELANGE.

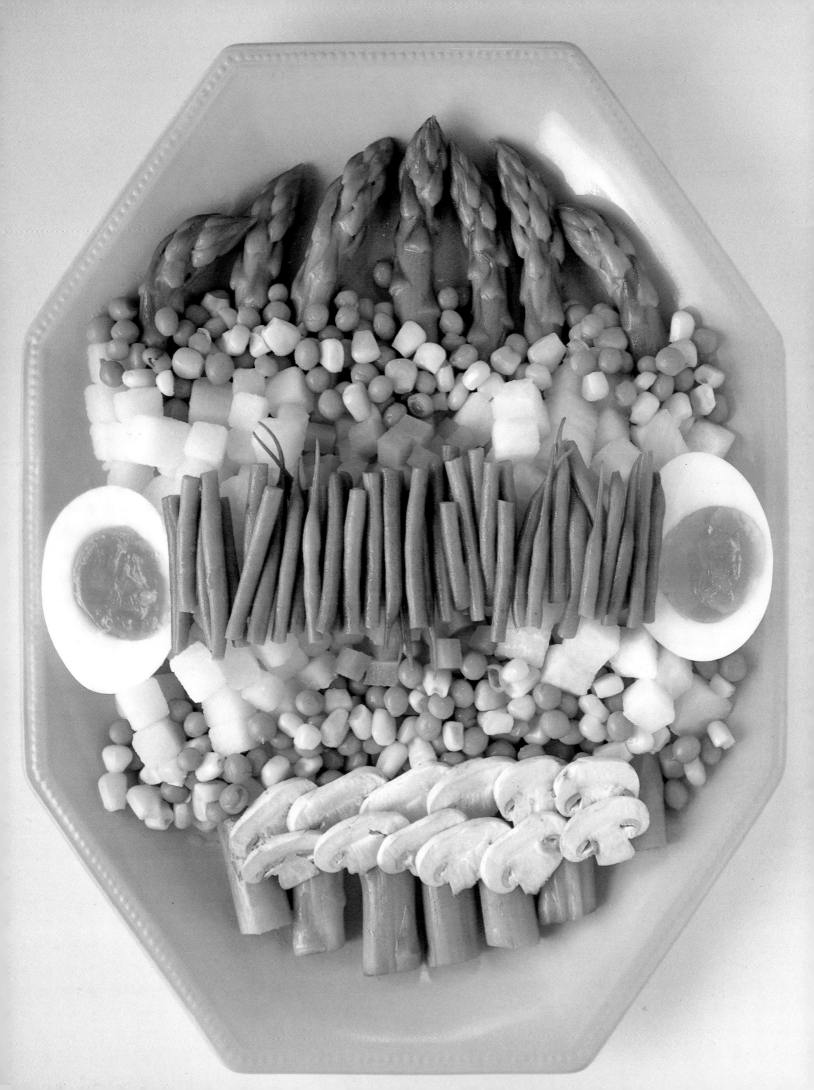

DRESSING

½ cup mayonnaise □ ½ cup fromage frais □ 1 tsp Dijon mustard □ 1 shallot, finely chopped □ 1 tbsp chopped parsley □ 2 hard-boiled eggs, quartered □ 2oz mushrooms, sliced

---

Trim the asparagus and steam for about 8 minutes or until just tender. Blanch the green beans, peas and sweetcorn in boiling water for about 4 minutes.

Dice the carrots, potatoes and turnips and cook in boiling water for 5–6 minutes. Drain all the vegetables and refresh under cold water. Leave to dry. Chill in the refrigerator.

Mix all the dressing ingredients together and spoon over the vegetables. Garnish with hard-boiled eggs and sliced mushrooms.

WARM CHICKEN SALAD

An elegant dish to prepare with economical chicken thighs, and one that is certain to be a favorite first course for dinner parties.

INGREDIENTS
---

3 chicken thighs, skinless and boneless □ 2 tbsps oil □ 1 clove garlic, peeled □ Small piece fresh ginger, peeled □ Salt and pepper □ 1 small frisee (curly endive), washed and dried □ 4oz lamb's lettuce (maché), washed and dried □ 3 tbsps tarragon vinegar □ 3 tbsps walnut oil

---

Cut the chicken into 1 inch pieces. Heat the oil in a saute pan with the garlic and ginger and add the chicken. Cook slowly until the chicken is tender. Sprinkle with salt and pepper, cover and keep warm.

Tear the frisee into bite-sized pieces and break the lamb's lettuce into separate leaves. Toss together in serving bowls. Remove the garlic and ginger from the chicken and discard them. Add the chicken and the oil left in the pan to the salad leaves. Mix the vinegar and walnut oil together and pour over the salads, toss and serve warm.

Facing page: WARM CHICKEN SALAD.

SALAD BOUQUETS

Flowers to eat? They are perfectly alright, especially if they're nasturtiums, with their lively, peppery taste and vibrant colors.

───────────── INGREDIENTS ─────────────

1 bunch watercress, washed ☐ 1 head oakleaf lettuce, washed ☐ 1 small iceberg lettuce, washed ☐ 12 nasturtium leaves and flowers ☐ Dandelion leaves or lamb's lettuce (mache) ☐ $1/3$ cup oil ☐ 2 tbsps lemon juice ☐ Pinch sugar, salt and pepper ☐ Chopped parsley

──

Remove thick stems and roots from the watercress. Break up the leaves into small sprigs. Break up the lettuces into bite-size pieces and leave the leaves whole.

Pile the watercress, lettuces and leaves onto plates and place the flowers in the center. Mix all the dressing ingredients and spoon over the salads.

SERVES 6

SALAD WITH CRISPY DUCK CROUTONS

Duck skin, when it is crisp and crunchy, is an out-of-this-world delicacy. Its richness is offset by the slightly bitter taste of endive and a tart dressing.

───────────── INGREDIENTS ─────────────

1 head curly endive ☐ Skin from 2 duck breasts ☐ 2 tbsps red wine vinegar ☐ $1/3$ cup olive oil ☐ 1 clove garlic, crushed ☐ $1/4$ tsp Dijon mustard ☐ Salt and pepper

──

Wash the endive and drain well. Tear the leaves into bite-size pieces. Refrigerate until needed.

─────────────────────────────

Facing page: SALAD BOUQUETS.

Above: SALAD WITH CRISPY DUCK CROÛTONS.

Cut the duck skin into thin strips. Place in a roasting pan and sprinkle with salt. Place in a preheated 400°F oven and roast until crisp. Drain the fat frequently as the skin cooks.

Drain the duck crôutons on paper towels and keep warm. Mix the vinegar, oil, garlic and mustard together. Add freshly ground pepper and toss with the endives. Sprinkle the salad with warm duck crôutons and serve immediately.

SERVES 4–6

*V*EGETABLE SALAD IN LETTUCE BOATS

Crisp Romaine lettuce forms edible 'dishes' for this unusual salad combination of peas, carrots, celery and plantains (cooking bananas).

INGREDIENTS
---

3 carrots ☐ 6oz frozen peas ☐ 4 sticks celery ☐ 3 plantains or ripe
bananas ☐ Juice and grated rind of 1 lime ☐ 12 Romaine lettuce leaves,
washed and dried ☐ ½ cup mayonnaise ☐ 2 tsps honey ☐ Milk

Peel and dice the carrots, place in a saucepan of cold water, cover and
bring to the boil. Cook about 2 minutes. Cook the peas separately for
about 1 minute, drain and rinse under cold water. Leave to drain dry.

Dice the celery the same size as the carrots and slice the plantains or
bananas on the diagonal. Toss the slices in a little lime juice to prevent
discoloration. Arrange the salad ingredients on top of the lettuce leaves on
serving plates.

Mix remaining lime juice and the rind with the mayonnaise, honey
and enough milk to bring the dressing to coating consistency. Drizzle over
the salads and serve.

SERVES 6

Above: VEGETABLE SALAD IN LETTUCE BOATS.

PINEAPPLE PRINCESS SALAD

This refreshing salad offers a taste of the tropics with pineapple and mango. Both blend wonderfully with figs, soy sauce and sweet chutney dressing.

───────── INGREDIENTS ─────────

4oz fresh spinach leaves □ 1 small head lettuce, leaves separated □ 1 head radicchio, leaves separated □ 2oz fresh bean sprouts □ 1 small pineapple, peeled, cored and sliced □ 1 ripe mango, peeled and diced □ 2 figs □ ½ cup cottage cheese

───────── DRESSING ─────────

1 cup yogurt □ 1 tbsp sweet mango chutney □ 1 tbsp soy sauce □ Juice and grated rind of ½ an orange □ 1 tsp grated fresh ginger □ Salt and pepper

Above: PINEAPPLE PRINCESS SALAD.

Wash the salad leaves and pat dry. Arrange on a large serving plate. Blanch the bean sprouts for 20 seconds in boiling water, rinse under cold water and pat dry.

Place sliced pineapple and diced mango on top of the salad leaves. Place bean sprouts next to the pineapple.

Cut the figs in thirds and arrange 3 pieces at either end of the plate. Spoon the cottage cheese around the diced mango.

Mix the dressing ingredients together well in a food processor and pour into a small serving dish.

SERVES 6

Salad of crab, pate and orange

What seems like an odd combination of ingredients turns out to be a delightful one. It's a salad that can also be a main course.

INGREDIENTS

12 crab claws □ 6oz pate de foie gras with truffles □ 3 oranges □ Lemon juice □ 1 shallot, finely chopped □ ⅓ cup walnut oil □ 1 head radicchio □ 8oz frisee (curly endive) □ 8oz lamb's lettuce (mache) □ ½ bunch watercress □ 4oz cherry tomatoes

Remove the crab from the shells, trying to keep the claws whole. Cut the pate into 12 slices.

Peel and segment the oranges over a bowl to catch the juice. Make up to 3 tbsps with lemon juice, if necessary. Mix with the shallot and walnut oil.

Rinse all the salad greens and pat dry. Line a serving dish with the radicchio leaves and combine frisee, lamb's lettuce and watercress in the centre. Toss with the orange segments, tomatoes and half of the dressing. Add the crab claws and pate and spoon over the remaining dressing to serve.

SERVES 4–6

Chapter 5
PICNICS AND BARBECUES

MARINER'S KEBABS

Fish and seafood cooked outdoors is delicious. Meaty fish such as salmon, monkfish and swordfish take particularly well to grilling, as do succulent scallops.

———————————— INGREDIENTS ————————————

½ cup olive oil ☐ ⅓ cup white wine ☐ 2 tbsps lemon juice ☐ Salt and pepper ☐ 1 clove garlic, crushed ☐ ½ tsp ground coriander ☐ 1 tbsp coriander leaves, roughly chopped ☐ 2 leeks, trimmed and well washed ☐ 8 pea pods, topped and tailed ☐ 2 small onions, quartered ☐ 4 scallops, cut in half ☐ 1 salmon steak, cut 2 inches thick ☐ 12oz monkfish tail, skinned and boned ☐ 1 tuna or swordfish steak, cut 2 inches thick

Combine the oil, wine, lemon juice, seasoning, garlic, ground coriander and coriander leaves in a shallow dish.

Blanch the leeks in boiling water for about 1 minute. Drain well and cut into 4 pieces.

Blanch the pea pods briefly in boiling water, taking care not to overcook. Carefully cut down the length of one side and open out.

Cut the monkfish tail into pieces approximately the same size as the other fish and place in the marinade with all the other ingredients. Marinate in the refrigerator for at least 2 hours.

Wrap each piece of salmon in a pea pod and thread all the ingredients on long skewers, alternating the different types of fish and vegetables.

Cook over moderately hot coals, turning and basting often with the marinade for about 15 minutes.

SERVES 4

———————————————————————

Previous page: SPICED SMOKED LAMB, AVOCADO AND WALNUT SALAD, PASTA AND HAZELNUT SALAD and STRAWBERRY AND HONEY PANCAKES.
Facing Page: MARINER'S KEBABS.

PIQUANT GLAZED TROUT

A most unusual sauce for fish but a good one, this is particularly easy to make and especially good for barbecues.

INGREDIENTS
---

8 oz canned figs or plums □ 2 tbsps light brown sugar □ 2 tbsps cider vinegar □ Salt and pepper □ 4 cleaned trout, weighing about 8–10oz each □ 4 sprigs fresh rosemary □ 4 tbsps oil

---

Combine the figs or plums and their juice with the brown sugar, vinegar, salt and pepper in a medium saucepan and bring slowly to the boil. Allow to simmer gently for about 8–10 minutes until thick and syrupy. Break up the fruit as it cooks.

Make 3 cuts into the flesh on each side of the fish. Tuck a sprig of rosemary into the cavity of each fish and brush both sides of the fish with oil.

Place the fish over hot coals on a barbecue grill or under a preheated broiler for about 5–6 minutes per side, turning several times and basting with more oil, if necessary, to prevent sticking.

About 2 minutes before the end of cooking time, brush liberally with the fruit glaze on both sides of the fish. Allow the glaze to caramelize slightly. Serve immediately, with any remaining glaze used as a sauce.

SPICED POTATO KEBABS

This unusual treatment for new potatoes is perfect for summer barbecues, and just as good prepared under a broiler if it rains!

Facing page: PIQUANT GLAZED TROUT AND SPICED POTATO KEBABS.

—— INGREDIENTS ——

30 small, even-sized new potatoes, scrubbed □ Olive oil □ Ground cumin and coriander □ Ground mace and cinnamon □ Salt and pepper □ Pinch cayenne pepper □ Lemon juice

Cook the potatoes in boiling salted water for about 2 minutes and drain well.

Place the potatoes in a large bowl and pour over enough oil to coat them liberally. Add spices in quantities to suit your own taste. Season and add cayenne pepper and a dash of lemon juice.

Thread the potatoes onto oiled metal or wood skewers and cook under a preheated broiler or over hot coals until the skins crisp and the potatoes are tender. Brush with additional oil as needed. Serve immediately.

AVOCADO AND WALNUT SALAD

A double avocado treat, this salad makes a lovely first course or even a light lunch with style. Fresh ginger provides the right contrast to creamy avocado.

—— INGREDIENTS ——

4 avocados □ 4 tbsps oil □ Juice and grated rind of ½ lemon □ 1 tbsp tarragon vinegar □ 1 tsp freshly grated ginger □ Salt and pepper □ 1 small iceberg lettuce □ ¾ cup walnuts, roughly chopped □ Chopped fresh tarragon or chives

Cut 1 avocado in half and remove the stone. Peel and chop the flesh roughly. Place it in a food processor or blender with the oil, lemon juice and rind, vinegar, ginger, salt and pepper. Process until smooth.

Cut the remaining avocados in half, remove the stones, peel and slice. Cut the lettuce into 6 wedges, wash and pat dry. Combine avocados and lettuce in a serving bowl and spoon over the dressing. Sprinkle with chopped walnuts and tarragon or chives. Toss before serving.

SERVES 6

PASTA AND HAZELNUT SALAD

The fabulous taste of this pasta dish belies the simplicity of its preparation. It can be made in advance, which gives the flavors time to blend, and makes it taste even better.

--- INGREDIENTS ---

12oz spinach or plain tagliatelle □ ¾ cup hazelnuts □ 1/3 cup olive or nut oil □ 2 tbsps white wine vinegar □ ½ tsp Dijon mustard □ 1 tbsp chopped parsley □ 1 tbsp chopped fresh basil □ Pinch salt, pepper and sugar

Cook the pasta in boiling salted water until al dente. Rinse under hot water to remove the starch and then under cold water to chill. Drain well.

Toast the hazelnuts in a moderate oven until golden brown. Allow to cool, then chop.

Mix the remaining ingredients together well. Combine the pasta and nuts in a serving bowl and pour over the dressing. Toss well before serving.

SERVES 4–6

SPICED SMOKED LAMB

The sweet, rich taste of lamb combined with a smoky flavor is fabulous. While you can smoke the meat yourself, it can be ordered ready smoked from specialty shops and delicatessens.

--- INGREDIENTS ---

4 tbsps olive oil □ 2 tbsps white wine vinegar □ 1 clove garlic, crushed □ 1 inch piece fresh ginger, peeled and grated □ 1 tsp ground coriander □ Freshly ground black pepper □ 1 loin of smoked lamb, boned and rolled

Mix the oil, vinegar, garlic, ginger, coriander and pepper together to make a marinade.

Cut the lamb into 1½ inch slices and place in a shallow dish. Pour over the marinade and turn meat to coat all sides. Leave to marinate for 1 hour in the refrigerator.

Place the slices over hot coals on a barbecue grill and cook to desired doneness. Brush frequently with the marinade while cooking. The lamb can also be cooked under a preheated broiler.

SERVES 4–6

BANANAS BAKED WITH RUM AND CHESTNUTS

If a barbecued pudding sounds strange, reserve judgement until you taste this one. Once the coals have almost died down, these dessert parcels cook to perfection.

--- INGREDIENTS ---

4 bananas, peeled and halved □ Juice of 1 lemon □ 4 tbsps soft brown sugar □ ¼ cup sliced almonds □ 8oz canned chestnuts □ 4 tbsps dark rum

Place the bananas on pieces of foil large enough to wrap them up. Sprinkle with lemon juice and sugar.

Scatter the almonds and chestnuts on top. Drizzle with rum and seal the parcels.

If cooking on an outdoor barbecue grill, place the parcels at the sides where the heat is less intense, or wait until the coals have died down. Bake for 5–6 minutes.

The bananas may also be baked in a moderate oven for about 15 minutes. Serve warm with cream.

SERVES 4

STRAWBERRY AND HONEY PANCAKES

Make the most of strawberries by teaming them with these light little pancakes. Golden honey drizzled over them looks and tastes lovely.

─── INGREDIENTS ───

1 whole egg □ 1 egg yolk □ 1 tsp lemon rind □ 1 tbsp honey □ ¾ cup milk □ 1 cup all-purpose flour □ 1½ tsps baking powder □ 2 tbsps butter or margarine □ 1 tbsp brandy □ 8oz strawberries, hulled and sliced □ Oil for frying □ 1 cup heavy cream □ Additional honey to taste

Beat the whole egg, egg yolk, lemon rind and honey together. Add the milk the sift in the flour and baking powder gradually, beating well in between each addition to form a smooth batter. Fold in the melted butter or margarine.

Combine the brandy and strawberries and set aside. Brush a frying pan lightly with oil and place over high heat. Drop spoonfuls of batter onto the hot surface of the pan. Before the batter sets, arrange a few slices of strawberry on each pancake.

When the pancakes brown on the underside, turn over and brown the second side. Keep the pancakes warm while cooking the remaining batter.

Serve warm, drizzled with cream and additional honey.

SERVES 6–8

BOMBAY FISH PASTE FOR SANDWICHES

Have a tea party reminiscent of the days of the Raj. Something savory always goes so well with a good cup of tea.

3 tbsps butter or margarine □ 2 green onions, chopped □ 2 tbsps curry powder □ 14oz canned sardines, drained and boned □ 1 tbsp anchovy paste □ 1 tbsp mango chutney □ 1 hard-boiled egg □ Pinch cayenne pepper (optional)

Melt the butter or margarine in a small saucepan. Add the onions and cook to soften. Add the curry powder and cook slowly for about 2 minutes.

Add the sardines and break them up with a fork. Mix in the anchovy paste and mango chutney. Cook for a few minutes and then transfer to a food processor or blender.

Chop the hard-boiled egg roughly and add to the sardine mixture. Add cayenne pepper, if using, and process until smooth.

Use at room temperature on toast or muffins, or to fill brown bread sandwiches or Bridge Rolls.

FILLS 10 SANDWICH ROUNDS

JAMBON PERSILLE

A classic French dish made easy with the use of packet aspic and precooked ham. It's marvelous for summer lunches and equally good as an appetizer for a French menu anytime.

——————— INGREDIENTS ———————
4 cups made-up aspic □ $\frac{1}{3}$ cup dry white wine □ 1 tbsp gelatin □ 1½lbs cooked ham, diced □ 2 cloves garlic, finely chopped □ About 2 cups parsley, chopped

Make aspic according to directions. Pour wine into a small saucepan and sprinkle on the gelatin. Soak for 5 minutes then dissolve over low heat. Pour into the aspic.

Set the bowl of aspic into ice water and allow to thicken slightly. Stir in the ham, garlic and parsley. Pour into a dampened 3 pint mold and chill until very firm. Slice to serve.

Facing page: JAMBON PERSILLÉ.

CONTINENTAL COFFEE CAKE

The dark, rich color of Continental blend coffee enriches this quickly made cake packed with nuts and golden raisins. It's filled and topped with two different and delicious icings, too.

INGREDIENTS

1 heaped tbsp Continental blend instant coffee □ ⅓ cup boiling water □ 1 egg, beaten □ 4 tbsps honey □ 2½ cups all-purpose flour □ 1 tbsp baking powder □ Pinch salt and cinnamon □ 1 stick butter or margarine □ ½ cup packed dark brown sugar □ 2 tbsps chopped pecans □ 1 cup golden raisins

FILLING

4 tbsps butter □ 1 cup powdered sugar □ Few drops vanilla extract □ 4 tbsps chopped pecans

TOPPING

1 cup powdered sugar □ Reserved coffee □ Pecan halves

Mix the instant coffee with the boiling water and add 4 tbsps of the mixture to the egg and honey in a small bowl. Reserve the remaining coffee for later use.

Sift the flour and baking powder with a pinch of salt and cinnamon into a large bowl and rub in the butter until the mixture resembles fine breadcrumbs. Stir in the sugar.

Make a well in the center of the ingredients and pour in the coffee, honey and egg. Mix the ingredients together to dropping consistency. Add more water, if necessary. Mix in the pecans and golden raisins.

Oil an 8 inch round cake pan and place a circle of wax paper in the bottom. Lightly dredge the base and sides of the pan with flour, tapping out the excess. Spoon the mixture into the pan and smooth the top.

Bake in a preheated 325°F oven for about 1½ hours, or until the cake pulls away from the sides of the pan. Allow to cool slightly, loosen

Facing page: CONTINENTAL COFFEE CAKE.

from the pan and turn the cake onto a wire rack to cool completely.

Soften the butter for the filling and beat in the vanilla. Beat in the powdered sugar gradually and stir in the pecans. When the cake is cool, slice it in half horizontally and spread on the filling. Sandwich the two halves together.

To make the topping, sift the powdered sugar into a bowl, stir in the reserved coffee and add enough water to make a spreadable icing. Pour onto the top of the cake and spread out to the edges. Top with the pecan halves before the icing sets.

MAKES 1 CAKE

BLACK OLIVE LOAF

Olives are an unusual ingredient to add to bread. This loaf makes tasty sandwiches and is also delicious spread with cream cheese.

INGREDIENTS

4 cups flour □ Pinch salt and sugar □ 1 cup warm water □ 1 tbsp dry yeast □ 4oz black olives, pitted and roughly chopped □ Oil

Sift the flour with a pinch of salt and sugar into a large mixing bowl. Combine the yeast with 2 tbsps of the water and stir in 2 tbsps of the flour. Leave in a warm place until frothy.

Mix the remaining water with the remaining flour and stir in the yeast mixture until well blended. Turn the dough onto a floured surface and knead for about 10 minutes, working in the olives.

Place in a lightly oiled bowl and turn over to oil all surfaces. Cover the bowl with a damp cloth and set in a warm place until doubled in bulk.

Knock down the dough, knead lightly and shape into a loaf. Place in an oiled 1lb loaf pan and bake in a preheated 375°F oven for 1 hour. Turn out onto a wire rack to cool before slicing.

MAKES 1 LOAF

Facing page: BLACK OLIVE LOAF.

CELEBRATION SANDWICHES

These sandwiches are so pretty they demand a special occasion; perfect for a birthday, wedding or christening party.

―――――――――― INGREDIENTS ――――――――――

½ quantity St. Clement's Butter □ 1 cup cream cheese □ Pinch white pepper □ 1 tsp lemon juice □ 1 stick celery, finely diced □ 6oz shrimp, chopped □ 12 small strawberries □ 12 slices white bread, crusts removed

Prepare the flavored butter according to the recipe and leave at room temperature.

Soften the cream cheese and beat in the white pepper and lemon juice.

Stir in the celery and shrimp, mixing thoroughly. Hull the strawberries and rinse, if necessary. Slice them thinly.

Spread the slices of bread with the prepared butter. Spread the filling on half of the bread and layer the strawberries on top. Top with remaining bread and cut each sandwich into 4 triangles.

MAKES 24 TRIANGLES

EDWARDIAN SANDWICH FINGERS

Chicken and tongue combined in a sandwich was a favorite for tea in England's Edwardian days. These sandwiches get extra flavor from the savory butter and zippy mustard and cress.

―――――――――――

Facing page: EDWARDIAN SANDWICH FINGERS, SARDINIA ROUNDS and CELEBRATION SANDWICHES.

½ quantity Sherried Tomato Butter ☐ 8oz chicken
portions ☐ Mayonnaise ☐ Salt, pepper and nutmeg ☐ 16 thin slices brown
bread, crusts removed ☐ 8 thin slices smoked tongue ☐ 1 punnet mustard and
cress or ½ bunch watercress, washed

Prepare the flavored butter according to the recipe. Poach the chicken in a
saucepan with enough water to cover. Bring to the boil and then simmer
until tender. Cool completely and remove skin and bones. Shred the flesh
and combine with enough mayonnaise to moisten thoroughly. Add salt,
pepper and nutmeg to taste.

Spread the slices of bread with the flavored butter and place sliced
tongue on half the bread. Top with the chicken mayonnaise and spread it
out evenly. Add the cress and cover with the remaining slices of bread.
Slice each round into 3 fingers before serving.

MAKES 24 FINGERS

Sardinia Rounds

*A sandwich filling with an Italian flavor and an unusual blend of ingredients. They are
ingredients, though, that can easily be kept on hand.*

—— INGREDIENTS ——
½ quantity Italian Butter ☐ 8oz unsweetened canned chestnuts ☐ 8oz canned
sardines, drained and boned ☐ 1 tbsp capers, drained ☐ 12 slices white or
brown bread

Prepare the flavored butter and keep at room temperature.

Drain the chestnuts thoroughly and chop roughly. Place the sardines in a bowl and mash with a fork. Add the capers and chopped
chestnuts.

Cut the slices of bread in 4 inch rounds with a fluted pastry cutter.
Spread the rounds of bread with the Italian Butter and then top half of the
rounds with the sardine mixture. Top with remaining bread and serve.

MAKES 6 ROUNDS

FLAVORED BUTTERS

These butters give added interest to sandwiches and are easy to make. They can be prepared well in advance, too, and frozen for use anytime.

――――― INGREDIENTS ―――――

ST. CLEMENT'S BUTTER

2 sticks unsalted butter □ Juice and rind of ½ lemon □ Grated rind of 1 orange

LEMON MINT BUTTER

2 sticks unsalted butter □ Juice and rind of ½ lemon □ 4 tbsps chopped fresh mint

CHIVE AND PARSLEY BUTTER

2 sticks unsalted butter □ Juice and rind of ½ lemon □ 2 tbsps chopped chives □ 2 tbsps chopped parsley

ITALIAN BUTTER

2 sticks unsalted butter □ 1 tbsp chopped fresh basil □ 1 tbsp chopped fresh oregano or marjoram □ 1 tbsp chopped Italian parsley □ ½ clove garlic □ Dash lemon juice □ Salt and pepper

MUSTARD BUTTER

2 sticks unsalted butter □ 1½ tbsps whole grain mustard

SHERRIED TOMATO BUTTER

2 sticks unsalted butter □ 1 tbsp dry sherry □ 1½ tbsps tomato paste

PEPPERED WATERCRESS BUTTER

2 sticks unsalted butter □ ½ bunch watercress, washed and finely chopped □ 2 tsps crushed black peppercorns □ Dash lemon juice

Soften the butter before adding the chosen flavoring ingredients. The butter can be prepared in a food processor or with an electric mixer to make combining the ingredients easier.

Use the butter at room temperature or seal in small containers and refrigerate or freeze. Bring to room temperature before using.

MAKES 1 CUP OF EACH FLAVOR

SPICED MEAT POTS

As an appetizer, these little pots of spicy corned beef and tongue are easy to make and will keep for several days in the refrigerator under their layer of clarified butter.

───────────── INGREDIENTS ─────────────

12oz canned corned beef □ ½ quantity Mustard Butter □ 1 tsp allspice □ Pinch cayenne □ 1 tbsp dry sherry □ 4oz smoked tongue, diced □ 1 stick butter

Combine the corned beef, mustard butter, allspice and sherry in a food processor. Process once or twice to mix.

Stir in the diced tongue by hand and spoon the mixture into custard cups or a terrine. Smooth the top.

To clarify butter for sealing the meat, melt the butter in a small saucepan and bring it to the boil. Take off the heat and allow to settle. Skim the salt off the top and pour the buttery oil off carefully. Discard the milk solids in the bottom of the pan or save to use on hot vegetables.

Pour an even layer of clarified butter over the top of each custard cup or the terrine and refrigerate until the butter sets. Serve with toast, French bread or bridge rolls.

SERVES 6

BRIDGE ROLLS

These tender white rolls are perfect with sandwich fillings or just on their own with butter. Their shape makes them ideal for packing in picnic baskets.

───────────── INGREDIENTS ─────────────

⅓ cup milk □ ¼ tsp sugar □ 1 tbsp dried yeast □ 2 cups white bread flour □ Pinch salt □ 4 tbsps butter or margarine □ 2 eggs

Facing page: BRIDGE ROLLS – the perfect base for
FLAVORED BUTTERS and GINGERED SALMON ROLLS.
Top right: SPICED MEAT POTS.

Heat the milk until lukewarm, and mix it with the sugar and yeast. Leave the mixture in a warm place for about 15 minutes, or until frothy.

Sift the flour with the salt into a warm bowl and rub in the butter or margarine – this can also be done in a food processor. Add the yeast mixture along with one of the eggs. Mix to form a soft dough. Turn out onto a floured surface and knead for about 10 minutes, or until smooth and elastic.

Place the dough in a lightly-oiled bowl, cover and set in a warm place for about 2 hours, or until doubled in bulk. Punch down and knead again for about 5 minutes, or until smooth and not sticky.

Divide the dough into 18 equal pieces. Shape each piece into an oblong of about 1½–2 inches in length. Place the rolls about ½ inch apart on a lightly greased baking sheet, covered with oiled plastic wrap, and set in a warm place for a further 20–30 minutes, or until nearly doubled in size.

Beat the remaining egg with a pinch of salt and brush the tops of the rolls evenly. Bake in a preheated 425°F oven for about 20 minutes, or until golden brown. Cool on a wire rack.

MAKES 18

GINGERED SALMON ROLLS

Bridge rolls filled with fresh salmon combined with grated ginger and toasted almonds will be a sensation on any tea table.

--- INGREDIENTS ---

12 Bridge Rolls □ ½ quantity St. Clement's Butter □ 1 tbsp butter or margarine □ 3 tbsps sliced almonds □ 8oz salmon □ ½ inch piece fresh ginger, finely grated □ 1 tbsp sherry □ 1 small bayleaf

Prepare Bridge Rolls and St. Clement's Butter according to the recipes.

Melt the butter or margarine in a small frying pan and, when foaming, add the almonds. Cook over gentle heat, stirring frequently until golden brown. Remove from the heat and set aside.

Meanwhile, skin the salmon and remove any bones. Place in a small casserole with the ginger, sherry, bayleaf and enough water to just cover. Cover the casserole and poach in a 350°F oven for about 15 minutes, or until tender.

Allow to cool, then strain, reserving the liquid. Remove the bayleaf and mash the salmon roughly with a fork. Add some of the cooking liquid if the salmon seems dry.

Cut the Bridge Rolls almost in half and spread cut surfaces with the flavored butter. Fill with the gingered salmon and sprinkle each roll with the almonds. Fold over the top of each roll to serve.

MAKES 12 SANDWICHES

CHICKEN STUFFED WITH SMOKED SALMON

Served cold, this makes sophisticated picnic fare, perfect for an elegant al fresco meal. Served hot, it adds interest to a dinner party menu.

INGREDIENTS

6 chicken breasts, skinned and boned □ 8oz smoked salmon □ ½ cup cream cheese □ ½ tsp horseradish cream □ Juice of 1 lemon □ Butter □ Lamb's lettuce (mache) to garnish

Cut a pocket down the thicker side of each chicken breast. Combine the remaining ingredients, except the garnish, in a food processor and work to a purée. Fill a pastry bag fitted with a plain tube with the mixture and pipe into each pocket in the chicken.

Butter 6 pieces of foil large enough to wrap up each chicken breast. Place on the chicken and seal each parcel securely. Place in a roasting pan and bake in a preheated 350°F oven for about 30 minutes or until the chicken is completely cooked. Serve hot or cold on beds of lamb's lettuce.

SERVES 6

SPINACH PATE

This is a perfect first course for vegetarians or indeed for anyone who loves spinach. It packs well for picnics, too.

—————————————— INGREDIENTS ——————————————

1 lb fresh spinach, washed □ 2 eggs □ 1 tbsp lemon juice □ Pinch salt, pepper
and nutmeg □ 2 slices bread, crusts removed □ ¾ cup heavy cream □ 1 loaf
white bread, sliced □ Unsalted butter, softened

Cook the spinach in only the water that clings to the leaves after washing.
Once the leaves wilt, remove from the pan and rinse under cold water.
Squeeze the leaves dry and place the spinach in a food processor.

Add the egg, lemon juice, salt, pepper and nutmeg. Crumble in the
2 bread slices and process to a purée. Mix in the cream. Spoon the mixture
into a buttered terrine and smooth the top. Cover the pan with foil and
place it in another pan of hot water. Cook in a preheated 325°F oven for
about 1 hour or until firm. Cool in the pan and then refrigerate overnight.

To serve, butter the bread and cut off the crusts. Remove the pâté
from the terrine and slice it into 2 layers. Cut the layers into slices the same
size as the slices of bread. Place one layer of pâté on a slice of bread and cut
into 3–4 fingers.

Soften the remaining butter and fill a pastry bag fitting with a small
writing tube. Pipe lines of butter over the fingers of pâté. Chill to set the
butter and serve.

GOOSEBERRY

PRESERVES

The combination of gooseberries and elderflowers is traditionally English. The taste is like delicious muscat grapes. Longer boiling produces a rosy color.

Facing page: SPINACH PÂTÉ.

INGREDIENTS

3lbs gooseberries ☐ 5 elderflowers ☐ 4 cups water ☐ 3lbs preserving
sugar ☐ Lemon juice

Wash the gooseberries and pick over. Discard any overripe or damaged
berries. Place the gooseberries in a large, heavy-based saucepan. Rinse the
elderflowers well and wrap in cheesecloth, tying into a parcel. Place in the
saucepan with the gooseberries.

Pour in the water and bring slowly to the boil. Simmer gently until
the gooseberries soften. Add the sugar and stir to dissolve.

Bring the mixture back to the boil and allow to boil rapidly until the
jam reaches the setting point of 220°F on a sugar thermometer. If the jam
does not set, add lemon juice and re-boil.

Pour the jam into sterilized preserving jars and cover the surface of
the jam with wax discs. Allow to cool and cover.

*I*CED SUNSHINE TEA

*This tea 'brews' in the light of the sun. Made in the refrigerator, it will brighten up even
cloudy summer days.*

INGREDIENTS

½ cup granulated sugar ☐ 1 cup water ☐ Rind of 1 lemon, pith removed ☐ 3
tbsps Earl Grey tea leaves ☐ 4 cups cold water

Combine the sugar and water in a heavy-based saucepan and stir to mix.
Add the lemon rind and bring slowly to the boil, swirling the pan
occasionally to help dissolve the sugar.

Simmer until the sugar dissolves completely. Remove the lemon
rind and allow to cool. Store in the refrigerator.

To make the tea, combine the tea leaves and water in a glass jar.
Cover and set out in the sun for at least 5 hours. Alternatively, place in the
refrigerator overnight.

Facing page: GOLDEN RAISIN SCONES,
ICED SUNSHINE TEA, GOOSEBERRY PRESERVES
and SPICY LEMON BREAD.

Strain the tea and discard the leaves. Pour into a glass jug and add lemon sugar syrup to taste. Add ice and serve.

If desired, add fresh mint and lemon slices to the tea for extra flavor and an attractive look.

MAKES 4 CUPS

GOLDEN RAISIN SCONES

Teatime is just not complete without hot, freshly baked scones. Spread with jam, clotted cream or simply butter, they are delicious!

--- INGREDIENTS ---

2½ cups all-purpose flour □ 1 tbsp baking powder □ Pinch salt □ 1½ sticks butter or margarine □ 4 tbsps sugar □ 1 cup golden raisins □ 1 egg, beaten □ 2 tbsp milk

Sift the flour, baking powder and salt into a large bowl or process once or twice in a food processor. Rub in the butter or margarine until the mixture resembles fine breadcrumbs, or work in the food processor.

Stir in the sugar and golden raisins by hand. Add the egg and milk, mixing to a soft dough. Turn out onto a floured surface and knead lightly until smooth.

Roll out to a thickness of 1 inch. Cut into 2 inch rounds with a pastry cutter. Transfer to a lightly oiled baking sheet and place in a preheated 400°F oven for about 10–12 minutes. Remove to a wire rack to cool slightly. Serve warm.

MAKES 2 DOZEN

SPICY LEMON

BREAD

A light yeast bread with a lovely lemony taste, this is marvellous with both tea and coffee, and as irresistible as only fresh bread can be.

INGREDIENTS

1/3 cup lukewarm water □ 1 tbsp dry yeast □ 2 tbsps sugar □ 2 cups all-purpose flour □ Pinch salt □ 1 tsp mixed spice □ Grated rind and juice of 1 lemon □ 1 cup small raisins □ 1 egg, lightly beaten □ 1 cup powdered sugar □ Oil

---

Mix the warm water with the yeast and 1 tsp of the sugar. Leave in a warm place for about 15 minutes, or until frothy.

Sift the flour with a pinch of salt into a warm bowl and add mixed spice, lemon rind and raisins. Add the egg to the yeast mixture and stir it into the flour.

Turn the mixture out onto a floured surface and knead for about 10 minutes, or until smooth and elastic. Place in an oiled bowl, cover and set in a warm place for about 2 hours, or until doubled in bulk.

Punch the dough down and knead again for a few minutes. Divide the dough in half and shape each half into a loaf. Place each half in a well-oiled 1lb loaf pan, cover loosely and set in a warm place for about 20 minutes, or until the dough rises to the top of the pans.

Bake the loaves in a preheated 400°F oven for 30–40 minutes, or until golden brown on top. When the bread is done, the bottom of each loaf will sound hollow when tapped. Remove to a wire rack to cool.

To prepare the icing, sift the powdered sugar into a bowl and add the lemon juice. If necessary, add enough hot water to make a smooth icing. The icing should be thick enough to stay on the top of each loaf and drip slightly down the sides. Serve when the icing is set.

GLOUCESTER BISCUITS

These savory biscuits take their name from the cheese used to make them. They are tender, buttery and rich, and will disappear quickly.

INGREDIENTS

1½ cups all-purpose flour □ 1½ sticks butter or margarine □ 1½ cups grated Cheddar cheese, finely grated □ Pinch paprika □ Salt and pepper

---

Place the flour in the bowl of a food processor and process once or twice to sift. Cut the butter or margarine into small pieces and add to the flour. Process once or twice and add the cheese. Add paprika and seasonings and work to a stiff dough. Chill if necessary.

Turn the dough out onto a floured surface and roll out to a rectangle about ⅓ inch thick. Cut into rounds with a 1½ inch pastry cutter. Transfer to a baking sheet lined with non-stick baking paper and place in a preheated 400°F oven for about 10–12 minutes, or until lightly browned. Remove to a wire rack to cool.

MAKES 30–36

Pate en Gelee

Pâtés are always popular and are so easy to take on a picnic. They can be prepared in advance and, if sealed with aspic or clarified butter, will keep very well.

INGREDIENTS

12oz unsmoked bacon, chopped □ 1lb ground pork □ 1 small onion, finely chopped □ 6 slices bread, made into crumbs □ 2 hard-boiled eggs, chopped □ 2 eggs, beaten □ Salt and pepper □ Pinch nutmeg □ 2 tsp chopped fresh thyme □ 1 packet aspic □ 2 tbsps sherry □ Bay leaves and juniper berries to decorate

Combine all the ingredients except the aspic, sherry and decoration. Mix very well until completely blended. Press into a 2lb terrine and cover tightly with the lid or with foil. Place in a roasting pan with enough hot water to come halfway up the sides of the terrine.

Bake in a preheated 325°F oven for about 1¼–1½ hours or until the juices run clear. Weight down the top and cool at room temperature. Refrigerate until firm and completely cold.

Prepare the aspic according to the package directions. Add the sherry and place the mixture in ice water until syrupy. Uncover the pâté and spoon over a layer of aspic. Chill until set. Decorate with bay leaves and juniper berries and set with a thin layer of aspic. Fill the terrine to the top with aspic and chill. Serve with melba toast.

Facing page: PÂTÉ EN GELÉE.

SAUCISSON EN BRIOCHE

A favorite French snack, this rich brioche loaf, stuffed with garlic or spicy sausage, is such a satisfying treat.

INGREDIENTS

3 cups flour □ 1 tsp salt □ 1½ tbsps yeast □ 5ml/1 tsp sugar □ ⅓ cup warm milk □ 2 eggs, beaten □ 4 tbsps butter □ 1 long garlic or spicy sausage, skinned □ 1 egg, beaten with a pinch of salt

Sift the flour into a warm bowl with a pinch of salt. Mix the yeast and sugar and combine with the milk and eggs. Add to the flour and beat well.

Soften the butter and beat it into the dough, bit by bit. Cover the bowl and leave for about 40 minutes in a warm place for the dough to rise.

Divide the dough in half. Press half into a well-greased 1lb loaf pan. Sprinkle the sausage with flour and place on top of the dough down the center of the pan. Top with the remaining dough and leave to rise in a warm place until the dough fills the pan.

Brush the top of the loaf with beaten egg glaze and bake in a preheated 425°F oven for about 45 minutes, or until the top of the loaf is golden brown. Remove to a wire rack to cool.

MAKES 1 LOAF

Facing page: SAUCISSON EN BRIOCHE.

Chapter 6

MEAT AND
POULTRY

LAMB CASSIS

The rich, slightly sweet taste of lamb goes well with a fruit sauce. Blackberries, when available, make a lovely alternative to blackcurrants.

───────────── INGREDIENTS ─────────────

2 loins of lamb, boned □ ½ pint oil □ Juice of 2 lemons □ 2 allspice berries □ 1 bay leaf □ 4 tbsps butter □ 8oz fresh, frozen or canned blackcurrants □ Pinch sugar, salt and pepper □ 3 tbsps creme de cassis □ 1 tbsp brandy □ 2 tbsps unsalted butter □ 3 dessert apples, peeled, halved and cored □ 18 chestnuts, peeled and cooked

───────────────────────────────────────

Remove all the outside fat from the lamb, leaving only the eye of the meat. Combine the oil, lemon juice, allspice berries and bay leaf. Place the meat in a shallow pan and pour over the marinade. Turn several times to coat, and leave to stand 2–3 hours, turning occasionally.

After marinating, remove the lamb and dry on paper towels. Reserve the marinade. Heat 1 tbsp of butter in a frying pan and when foaming place in 1 loin. Cook over high heat, turning to sear all the sides. If the butter blackens, wipe out the pan and add fresh butter. Repeat with the second loin and then cook both to the desired doneness.

Keep the meat warm and deglaze the pan with some of the reserved marinade. Add the blackcurrants with their juice if frozen or canned. For fresh blackcurrant add about ⅓ cup water. Cook until the currants soften, and stir in the sugar. Bring to the boil and season with salt and pepper. Add the cassis and brandy and set the sauce aside.

Melt the unsalted butter in a frying pan and, when foaming, place in the apples, rounded side down. Cook slowly until light golden brown, then turn over. Cook until just tender and slightly translucent. Remove the apples and cook the chestnuts until soft. Slice the apples thinly, leaving them attached at the top.

To serve, slice the lamb into ¼-inch-thick slices. Spoon blackcurrant sauce onto serving plates and arrange slices of lamb on top. Spoon on a few chestnuts and add the apples. Carefully press the apples so that they open like fans.

SERVES 6

─────────────────────────────

Facing page: LAMB CASSIS.

ROLLED PORK LOIN WITH HERB AND MUSHROOM STUFFING

When thinking of elegant food, pork is not one of the things that springs to mind first. However, a rolled loin with a flavorful stuffing can be truly 'upmarket'.

INGREDIENTS

4½lbs whole loin of pork, boned and trimmed.

STUFFING

4oz cup mushrooms □ 6 green onions, chopped □ 2 tsps chopped fresh basil □ 2 tsps chopped fresh parsley □ 1 clove garlic, crushed □ Salt and pepper □ Pinch nutmeg □ 4 slices bread, made into crumbs □ 8oz sausage meat □ 1 egg, beaten

SAUCE

1 cup chicken stock □ 2 tsps cornstarch □ 4 tbsps dry sherry □ ½ cup raisins □ 2 tbsps capers

Make sure all the fat is removed from inside the pork loin and leave only a thin layer on the outside. Cut into the middle of the eye of the meat but not all the way through. Open out the cut portion and flatten it.

Mix the stuffing ingredients together and form into a sausage shape along the eye of the meat. Roll the meat around the stuffing to enclose it completely. Tie the roll at 1 inch intervals with fine string.

Cover with foil and place in a roasting pan in a preheated 400°F oven for 20 minutes per per pound and 20 minutes over. Uncover during the last 20–30 minutes of cooking to brown the fat. Make sure the juices

Facing page: ROLLED PORK LOIN WITH HERB AND MUSHROOM STUFFING.

run clear and the stuffing is thoroughly cooked before removing the meat from the oven. Allow to stand 10–15 minutes before slicing.

Skim the fat from the pan juices. Discard the fat and mix the juices with the stock, cornstarch and sherry. Bring to boil in a small saucepan, stirring continuously. Add the raisins and capers and cook the sauce until thickened and clear. Serve over the slices of stuffed pork.

SERVES 6

DEVILLED KIDNEYS AND MUSHROOMS

A good dish for breakfast, brunch, lunch or a light supper, these kidneys have a deliciously spicy sauce. This dish is also very quick to prepare.

INGREDIENTS

12oz canned tomatoes □ 16 lamb's kidneys, skinned □ 3 tbsps oil □ 2 tsps hot curry powder □ 1 tbsp paprika □ 3 tbsps white wine vinegar □ 1 tbsp Worcestershire sauce □ 1 tbsp mango chutney □ 6oz button mushrooms □ Pinch salt and pepper

Purée the tomatoes and their juice in a food processor and push through a sieve to remove the seeds. Set aside.

Cut the kidneys in half and remove the cores with scissors. Heat the oil in a large frying pan and add the kidneys, rounded side down first. Cook over high heat to seal both sides. Remove to a plate.

Add the curry powder and paprika to the pan and cook briefly. Add the vinegar, Worcestershire sauce, chutney and puréed tomatoes. Bring to the boil and allow to cook rapidly for a few minutes.

Rinse the mushrooms, if necessary, and add to the sauce. Cook for 2 minutes and then return the kidneys to the pan. Simmer for about 12–15 minutes, or until the kidneys are tender. Do not allow the kidneys to boil rapidly in the sauce. Taste and season with salt and pepper before serving.

Facing page: DEVILLED KIDNEYS AND MUSHROOMS.

TURKEY RING WITH RICH WINE SAUCE

Anytime there is leftover turkey, there is a need for new ideas to use it creatively and deliciously. When the recipe is this good, you might want to cook turkey especially for it!

INGREDIENTS

1½lb cooked turkey □ 3 tbsps fresh breadcrumbs □ 1 cup milk □ 6 eggs □ 2 tsp chopped fresh thyme □ ½ tsp sage □ Pinch nutmeg □ Pinch salt and pepper □ Oil

SAUCE

3 tbsps butter □ 6oz mushrooms, quartered □ 1 shallot, finely chopped □ 1 cup stock □ ½ cup red wine □ 3 tbsps cranberry sauce □ 2 tbsps cornstarch □ 4 tbsps port □ ¾ cup walnuts □ Fried bread croutons (optional)

Remove skin and bones from the turkey and process the meat until finely chopped. Mix with the breadcrumbs, milk, eggs, herbs, nutmeg and seasoning.

Oil a 9 inch ring mold and spoon in the turkey mixture, press down well to eliminate air pockets. Smooth the top and place the mold in a bain marie. Bake in a 325°F oven for about 40 minutes or until a skewer inserted into the mixture comes out clean.

To make the sauce, melt the butter and cook the mushrooms and shallot until tender. Pour on the stock and wine and add the cranberry sauce. Simmer until the alcohol evaporates from the wine.

Mix the cornstarch with the port and add to the sauce. Bring to the boil, stirring constantly. Cook until the sauce thickens and clears. Add the walnuts.

Turn the turkey ring out onto a serving plate and fill the center with the sauce. Arrange the fried bread croutons around the ring, if desired.

SERVES 6

Facing page: TURKEY RING WITH RICH WINE SAUCE.

ROAST DUCK WITH SHALLOTS AND SALSIFY

Salsify is a vegetable that deserves to be more popular. It has a delicious taste and texture and goes very well with poultry or game.

INGREDIENTS

5lb duck □ 4oz puff pastry □ 1 egg, beaten with a pinch of salt □ 6 shallots, peeled □ 4 roots salsify, peeled and cut into 2 inch pieces □ Sugar □ 1 cup stock □ 4 tbsps brandy or sherry □ 2 duck livers □ Salt and pepper □ Chopped parsley

Remove any fat from inside the duck cavity. Prick the skin with a fork and sprinkle the skin with salt. Place the duck on a roasting rack in a preheated 400°F oven for 30 minutes, turning once.

Above: ROAST DUCK WITH SHALLOTS AND SALSIFY.

Drain off the fat and turn the duck again. Reserve about 4 tbsps of the duck fat. Raise the oven temperatures to 425°F and continue to cook the duck, turning twice more.

Roll out the puff pastry and brush with egg glaze. Cut into diamond shapes and place on a baking sheet. Make a lattice pattern on top of each diamond and bake along with the duck until golden brown. Remove to a wire rack.

Heat half the reserved duck fat in a heavy-based saucepan. Add the shallots and salsify with a pinch of sugar. Cover the pan and cook over high heat, shaking the pan constantly until the vegetables are tender and glazed. Set aside.

Remove the duck from the oven and cut off the legs. Return them to the oven to crisp the skin. Drain all the fat from the roasting pan and pour in the stock. Bring to the boil, scraping the meat juices from the bottom of the pan. Strain into a saucepan, add the brandy or sherry and boil rapidly to reduce and thicken the liquid.

Cook the livers quickly in the remaining duck fat and set aside. To assemble the dish, slice the duck breasts into thin slivers and leave the legs whole.

Arrange the breast meat in a fan shape on serving plates and place a leg at the top of the fan. Place the shallots and salsify in the center of each plate. Slice the livers into six pieces and arrange opposite the duck. Top the livers with puff pastry. Spoon over the sauce and garnish with chopped parsley.

ELEGANT TURKEY PIE

Pre-prepared puff pastry makes this pie exceptionally easy to put together. Two sauces with distinctively different tastes make it an extraordinary pie.

INGREDIENTS

3lbs boned turkey meat, white and dark □ ⅓ cup butter or margarine □ 3 shallots, finely chopped □ 1 tsp chopped fresh sage □ ½ cup stock □ 4 tbsps dry sherry □ 4oz flat mushrooms □ Salt and pepper □ 1lb puff pastry □ 1 egg, beaten with a pinch of salt

─────── GARNISH ───────

3 large turnips □ 8oz fresh spinach, washed □ 2 tbsps butter □ Pinch salt,
pepper and nutmeg

─────── SAUCES ───────

2 tbsps oil □ 2 shallots, finely chopped □ 1 tbsp flour □ 1 cup stock □ 4 tbsp
red wine □ 4 tbsps dry white wine □ 1½ sticks unsalted butter
□ Dash lemon juice

Cut the turkey into thin strips, keeping the white and dark meats separate. Melt the butter or margarine in a small pan and cook the shallots until softened. Add the sage, stock and sherry and bring to the boil. Boil rapidly a few minutes to reduce.

Cut the stems off the mushrooms and slice the caps. Sprinkle the turkey with salt and pepper.

Divide the pastry almost in half and roll out the smaller piece to a circle about 12 inches in diameter. Place on a lightly oiled baking sheet. Place a layer of dark turkey meat on the pastry to within ½ inch of the edges. Mix the white meat with the reduced stock and the mushrooms. Spread this over the dark meat and top with more dark meat.

Roll out remaining pastry to a circle about 1 inch larger in diameter than the base. Brush the edges of the pastry base with egg and place on the pastry top. Press the edges together to seal and trim neatly. Make a steam hole in the top of the pastry and use a sharp knife to carve a decorative pattern on the top without cutting all the way through.

Bake the pie in a preheated 375°F oven for about 35–40 minutes or until meat juices run clear. Keep warm in a low oven.

To prepare the garnish, peel the turnips and cut them in half. Shape into cups and use a cannelle knife to carve a pattern in the sides, if desired. Carefully hollow out their centers. Place in boiling water for about 4 minutes or until tender. Drain, cover and keep warm.

Cook the spinach in only the water that clings to the leaves after washing. When just wilted, remove from the heat and press the leaves dry. Chop finely and return to the saucepan with the butter and nutmeg. Cook over high heat to evaporate any remaining moisture. Cover and keep warm.

To prepare the sauces, heat the oil in a small saucepan and add the shallot. Cook slowly to soften. Add the flour and cook to brown, stirring

─────────────

Previous page: ELEGANT TURKEY PIE.

constantly. Pour on the stock, add the red wine and bring to the boil. Simmer about 10 minutes or until thickened.

Heat the white wine in a separate pan and whisk in the butter bit by bit. Do not allow the sauce to boil. Add lemon juice to taste and a pinch of salt and pepper.

To serve, pour the red wine sauce on half of each plate and the white wine sauce on the other. Reheat the garnish, if necessary, and place 1 filled turnip half on each plate. Slice the pie and place 1 slice on each plate. Serve the rest separately.

SERVES 6

*L*AMB AND TURNIPS FILLED WITH SPRING VEGETABLES

Turnips form 'containers' for a variety of spring vegetables to create an accompaniment for a special lamb dish. Dinner guests will be fascinated!

INGREDIENTS

2 best ends of lamb □ Oil □ ½ cup stock □ 1 sprig fresh rosemary □ ¼ tsp tomato paste □ 4 tbsps butter □ Salt and pepper □ 4 turnips, peeled □ 4 baby carrots, peeled □ 4 asparagus □ 4 broccoli flowerets □ 1 small beet, cooked and diced □ Small bunch tarragon

Remove all the fat and bones from the lamb, leaving only the eye of the meat. Slice this into pieces about ½ inch thick. Heat a small amount of oil in a frying pan and add a few slices of lamb. Press down to sear one side, turn over and sear the other side. Remove the lamb and continue until all the meat is cooked. Set it aside.

Deglaze the pan with the stock, and add the rosemary and tomato paste. Set aside.

Leave the green tops on the turnips. Blanch in boiling water until just barely tender. Cut in half and carefully scoop out part of the base to

Above: Lamb and Turnips filled with Spring Vegetables.

form a cup. Blanch the other vegetables, except the beet, until just tender. Chop beet finely. Melt half the butter and add 2 tsps chopped tarragon. Reserve 4 small tarragon sprigs. Pour the butter over the vegetables.

Bring the stock to the boil in the frying pan and when slightly reduced, return the meat to the pan to heat through. Remove the meat and rosemary from the sauce and whisk in the remaining butter. Season with salt and pepper to taste.

Spoon the sauce onto the plates and arrange lamb on top. Place the bottom halves of the turnips on the plates and fill with the vegetables. Place on the turnip tops and garnish with tarragon leaves.

SERVES 4

DUCK A LA RUSSE

A very unusual first course, this could also make a very special light supper. Beets and duck make an interesting flavor combination.

―――――――――――――――― INGREDIENTS ――――――――――――――――

2 duck breasts □ 1 cup sour cream □ 4 cooked beets, peeled □ 1/3 cup port □ 1 clove garlic, crushed □ Salt and pepper □ Sprigs of fresh dill

Place the duck in a roasting pan and sprinkle the skin with salt. Place in a preheated 425°F oven and cook until the skin is crisp, but the flesh is still slightly pink. Set aside to cool and then cut into thin slivers.

Place 1/3 cup of the sour cream in a food processor and add half of the beets. Purée until smooth. Purée the remaining beets with the port. Mix the remaining sour cream with the garlic.

Place the slices of duck breast in shallow serving bowls. Spoon in the garlic sour cream. Top with the beet-sour cream purée and then the beet-port purée. Garnish with dill and serve slightly chilled.

SERVES 6

MARINATED GRILLED DUCK

Grilled duck, especially when its cooked over coals, needs precooking for the best results. A good marinade is especially important for flavor and moisture.

―――――――――――――――― INGREDIENTS ――――――――――――――――

2 ducks, quartered □ 2 cups dry white wine □ 1 tbsp green peppercorns □ 2 cloves garlic, crushed □ 1 bouquet garni (bay leaf, parsley stalks and sprig thyme)

―――――――― DUCHESS POTATOES ――――――――

6 medium potatoes, peeled □ 2 eggs, separated □ Salt and white pepper □ Melted butter

--------- SAUCE ---------
1 tbsp softened butter □ 1 tbsp flour □ ¹/₃ cup heavy cream
--------- GARNISH ---------
Tomato roses, fennel and puff pastry crescents

Place the ducks in a roasting pan, skin side up. Combine the wine, peppercorns, garlic and bouquet garni and pour over. Roast, uncovered, in a preheated 400°F oven for about 30 minutes. Remove the breasts and continue to cook the legs another 15 minutes. Return the breasts to the pan and leave the duck to marinate in the juices for at least 4 hours.

Above: MARINATED GRILLED DUCK.

While the ducks are cooking, cut the potatoes in even-size pieces and place in cold, salted water. Cover, bring to the boil and cook about 20 minutes or until soft. Drain and place over high heat for a few minutes to dry. Mash until smooth.

Beat the egg whites until stiff but not dry. Beat the yolks and fold in the whites. Season with salt and pepper and pipe onto a lightly oiled baking sheet. Drizzle with melted butter. Bake in a preheated 325°F oven until risen and golden brown on the edges.

Remove the ducks from the marinade, skim any fat from the surface of the liquid and reserve it. Place the ducks under a preheated broiler or on an outdoor barbecue broiler. Cook skin side down first until crisp and golden. Turn over and continue to cook until the duck is tender. Cook the ducks about 6 inches away from hot coals.

Boil the marinade and mix the butter and flour to a smooth paste. Add to the boiling marinade bit by bit until thickened sufficiently. Add the heavy cream and boil again for about 2 minutes. Strain, if desired.

Transfer the duck to a serving platter and put cutlet frills on the leg ends, if desired. Surround with the potatoes and garnish with tomato roses, fennel and pastry crescents.

SERVES 4

HERBED GRILLED LAMB

Grilled rib chops get a coating of herbs that makes them moist and flavorful. This recipe is delicious cooked on a barbecue grill, too.

INGREDIENTS
---

12 lamb rib chops □ Chopped mixed fresh herbs □ Lemon juice □ Oil □ Pepper □ 1 clove garlic, crushed □ Orange slices and fresh redcurrants for garnishing

---

Trim the chops, removing all but a thin layer of fat. Allow about 1 tbsp herbs per chop. Mix with enough oil and lemon juice to make a basting mixture. Add the garlic and pepper and brush the mixture on the lamb.

Place under a hot broiler and turn and baste often as the chops cook to the desired doneness.

Serve garnished with orange slices and small bunches of currants.

SERVES 6

Facing page: HERBED GRILLED LAMB.

SPINACH MOLD BOLOGNESE

Italian meat sauce doesn't always need spaghetti to go with it. A creamy spinach mixture makes for an interesting combination.

―――――――― INGREDIENTS ――――――――

2lbs spinach □ 2 tbsps butter □ 2 tbsps flour □ 1 cup milk □ Salt, pepper and nutmeg □ 2 slices bread, made into crumbs □ 1 egg □ 12oz ground beef or veal □ 1 small onion, finely chopped □ 14oz canned tomatoes □ 1 tbsp tomato paste □ 1 tbsp chopped basil □ 2 tsps chopped oregano □ 1 bay leaf □ Salt and pepper □ Pinch sugar

Wash the spinach very well and cook in only the water that clings to the leaves. When just wilted, drain and squeeze dry. Place in a food processor and purée.

Melt the butter in a saucepan and stir in the flour off the heat. Gradually whisk in the milk and return to the heat. Bring to the boil, whisking constantly until thickened.

Combine with the spinach and add salt, pepper and a pinch of nutmeg. Add the breadcrumbs and egg and process until smooth. Spoon the mixture into a well buttered 2 pint ring mold, cover the top with foil and place in a roasting pan of warm water to come halfway up the sides of the mold. Bake in a preheated 350°F oven for about 1 hour, or until set.

To prepare the sauce, place the meat in a frying pan and cook slowly until the fat renders. Add the onion and brown quickly. Pour on the tomatoes and add the paste and remaining sauce ingredients. Cook very slowly for about 45 minutes.

Turn out the spinach mold onto a serving plate and spoon the sauce in the center and over the sides.

SERVES 6–8

Facing page: SPINACH MOLD BOLOGNESE.

CHICKEN CRECY

Crecy means the use of carrots in a recipe. In this case they are threaded through chicken breasts for a polkadot effect.

INGREDIENTS
---

6 even-sized chicken breasts □ 2 carrots, peeled □ 4 tbsps white wine □ 1 bay leaf □ 1 sprig thyme □ Salt and pepper □ 6 rashers bacon, rindless and boneless □ 2 heads chicory □ Lemon juice □ 2 sticks celery □ Chopped chives □ 1 small bunch watercress, well washed □ ½ cup mayonnaise □ ⅓ cup natural yogurt □ Pinch nutmeg

---

Pierce holes in each chicken breast. Slice carrots into thin strips and push them into the holes. Cut off the ends of the carrots level with the chicken.

Place chicken in a shallow dish and pour over the wine. Add enough water to cover and add the bay leaf and sprig thyme. Season lightly and poach in a moderate oven for about 15–20 minutes or until done.

Above: CHICKEN CRECY.

Remove the chicory cores and slice the leaves. Sprinkle with lemon juice and combine with the celery. Dice the bacon and cook slowly in a frying pan until the fat renders. Turn up the heat and brown. Mix with the chicory and celery. Add the chives, salt and pepper.

Remove any thick stems and the roots of the watercress and reserve a few leaves for garnishing. Purée the rest with the mayonnaise and yogurt in a food processor. Add seasoning to taste and a pinch of nutmeg.

To serve, pile some of the chicory, celery and bacon salad on a plate and add a chicken breast. Spoon on some of the watercress dressing and garnish the plate with reserved watercress leaves.

PIGEON NAVARIN

Use young pigeons for this warming casserole with lots of colorful vegetables and buttery sauce.

INGREDIENTS

4 pigeons, 6–8oz each □ 3½ cups stock □ Bouquet garni (bay leaf, sprig thyme, parsley stalks) □ 4 carrots, peeled and quartered □ 4 small parsnips, peeled and quartered □ 2 large turnips, peeled and shaped into barrels □ 2 leeks, cut in 4 pieces □ 2 zucchini, shaped into barrels □ 12 button onions, peeled □ 4 thick slices of bread, toasted □ 2oz beef marrow (optional) □ 4 tbsps dry white wine □ 1 stick unsalted butter □ Salt and pepper □ Chervil sprigs

Place the pigeons in a large saucepan and pour on the stock. Add the bouquet garni and bring to the boil. Simmer, covered, until the pigeons are tender.

Strain the stock into another saucepan, add the wine and bring to a rapid boil. Cook quickly to reduce by half. Meanwhile, place all the vegetables in a steamer and steam until just tender.

Add the bone marrow to the reduced stock and poach gently a few minutes. Remove the marrow and place one slice on each piece of toast and keep warm in a low oven.

Beat the butter into the hot stock, a small piece at a time, whisking constantly until thickened. Season to taste. Pour the sauce onto 4 plates and arrange vegetables on top. Quarter the pigeons and place the joints on top of the sauce. Add the marrow on toast and garnish with chervil.

Chapter 7

VEGETABLE FARE

STUFFED LEEKS

Layers of leeks are filled with a pork or chicken stuffing and served with an apricot sauce for an unusual dish.

———————————— INGREDIENTS ————————————

1 cup dried apricots, soaked □ 1 large leek □ 6oz pork or chicken, ground □ 1 tbsp chopped mint □ 1 tbsp chopped parsley □ Pinch nutmeg □ Salt and pepper □ 1 onion, chopped □ 3 tbsps rice □ Salt and pepper

Leave the apricots to soak until tender. Slice the leek almost in half lengthwise and rinse very well. Separate into about 12 layers.

Mix the pork or chicken, mint, parsley, nutmeg, seasoning, onion and rice and fill the leeks. Do not overfill; leave room for the rice to expand. Steam the leek rolls over simmering water for about 45 minutes.

Meanwhile, combine the apricots and enough water to cover in a small saucepan. Cook slowly until softened. If the rice does not cook in 45 minutes, steam for a further 15 minutes. Serve the stuffed leeks with the apricot sauce. Accompany with warm pitta bread.

SWEETCORN ALMONDINE

Baby sweetcorn has a delicate taste that blends well with interesting ingredients such as toasted almonds and fresh herbs. It's easy to cook and you can eat the whole cob!

———————————— INGREDIENTS ————————————

3 tbsps butter or margarine □ ¾ cup chopped or sliced almonds □ 1 tbsp chopped fresh herbs □ 2 tbsps grated Parmesan cheese □ 1 hard-boiled egg, chopped □ 32 baby sweetcorn ears □ Salt and pepper □ Dash light soy sauce (optional)

Previous page: SWEETCORN ALMONDINE.
Facing page: STUFFED LEEKS.

Melt the butter or margarine in a frying pan. Add the almonds and cook slowly to an even golden brown. Mix in the herbs, cheese and egg and set aside.

Trim the sweetcorn and cook in boiling salted water for about 4–5 minutes. Drain well and transfer to a serving dish. Drizzle with soy sauce, if desired and sprinkle over the topping. Season lightly and toss before serving.

SERVES 4

CREAMY MINTED LIMA BEANS

Yogurt and mint make a cool creamy sauce that is easy to prepare. While cornstarch will help stabilize the sauce, it still must not boil.

INGREDIENTS

3lbs fresh lima beans □ 1 cup chicken or vegetable stock □ ½ cup natural yogurt □ ¼ tsp cornstarch □ 1 tbsp lemon juice □ Salt and pepper □ 6–8 sprigs fresh mint

Remove the beans from their pods. Bring the stock to the boil in a large saucepan and add the beans. Cook about 5–6 minutes or until tender. Drain and reserve the stock. Remove the outer skins of the beans, if desired.

Boil the stock rapidly to reduce by about half. Mix the yogurt and the cornstarch and add to the stock gradually. Whisk well and bring almost to the boil for the cornstarch to thicken. Stir in the lemon juice and add seasoning to taste.

Shred only the leaves of the mint and stir into the sauce. Pour over the beans and serve immediately.

SERVES 4

Facing page: CREAMY MINTED LIMA BEANS.

CHICKPEA DIP

This excellent tasting dip for bread or raw vegetables can be made in a hurry with ingredients that will keep in any cupboard or refrigerator.

--- INGREDIENTS ---

15oz canned chickpeas, drained □ 1 clove garlic, peeled □ Juice of 1 lemon □ $^{1}/_{3}$ cup olive oil □ 2 tbsps sesame seeds □ Paprika and olives to garnish

Place all the ingredients in the bowl of a food processor and purée until smooth. Add more oil if the mixture is too thick.

Spoon into a bowl and sprinkle with paprika. Garnish with olives and serve with warm pitta bread or raw vegetables for dipping.

SERVES 8

BEETS CUMBERLAND

A classic Cumberland sauce with its slightly sweet-sour taste is the surprising sauce for these baby beets. The tastes complement each other wonderfully.

--- INGREDIENTS ---

20 small, fresh beets □ $^{1}/_{3}$ cup red wine □ Grated rind and juice of 1 orange □ 1 bouquet garni (bayleaf, parsley stalks, sprig thyme) □ Pinch allspice □ Salt and pepper □ 2 tbsps redcurrant jelly □ 1 tbsp red wine vinegar □ 1 tbsp port

Trim the beets and place, unpeeled, in a pan of cold water. Cover the pan and bring to the boil. Simmer gently for about 15–20 minutes, or until just tender.

Facing page: BEETS CUMBERLAND.

Drain and leave to cool slightly. Peel with a sharp knife. If the beets are very young, leave unpeeled, if desired.

While the beets are cooking, pour the wine into a medium saucepan. Add the orange rind and juice, bouquet garni, allspice and seasonings.

Bring to the boil and then simmer until reduced by half. Stir in the redcurrant jelly and vinegar. Bring back to the boil and cook briefly to melt the jelly and evaporate the vinegar. Stir in the port and remove the bouquet garni.

Allow to cool and pour over either hot or cold beets.

SERVES 4

PIQUANT MAYONNAISE FOR VEGETABLES

This versatile sauce can be served with fish, chicken and cold meats as well as vegetables. It's even delicious when the vegetables are hot!

INGREDIENTS

White of 1 hard-boiled egg, diced □ 1 tbsp chopped parsley □ 1 tsp chopped coriander □ 2 tbsps chopped capers □ 2 tsps white wine vinegar □ ½ tsp Dijon mustard □ Pinch sugar (optional) □ 1 cup mayonnaise □ 2lbs young vegetables such as zucchini, carrots, pea pods, green beans

Combine all the ingredients, except the vegetables and mix together well. Leave in the refrigerator at least 1 hour for the flavors to blend.

Prepare the vegetables and poach in boiling salted water for about 1–2 minutes depending on the vegetable. Rinse under cold water, drain well and pat dry. Serve with the sauce.

SERVES 6–8

MASHED PARSNIPS

Instead of potatoes, try a purée of parsnips as an accompaniment to roast meats, poultry, your favorite sausages, or use as a topping for shepherd's or fisherman's pie.

—————————————— INGREDIENTS ——————————————

1½lbs parsnips □ 1½ tbsps butter □ ½ cup all-purpose yogurt □ Salt,
pepper and nutmeg

Peel the parsnips and quarter them. Remove the cores and cut the parsnips into large pieces. Place in cold salted water to cover. Cover the pan and bring to the boil. Cook until tender.

Drain well and return to the saucepan. Mash over heat until dry. Beat in the butter and the yogurt. Add salt and pepper to taste along with a pinch of nutmeg. Serve immediately.

SERVES 6

CHIPPED PARSNIPS

Chips don't always have to mean potatoes. The sweet taste of parsnips is wonderful when crisply fried. Parsnips chips are especially good served with poultry or game.

—————————————— INGREDIENTS ——————————————

4 medium parsnips, peeled □ Oil for deep frying □ Salt

Cut the parsnips in half and trim off the narrow ends and reserve. Cut the thicker part into 6–8 wedges, depending on the thickness of the parsnips. If the cores are woody, trim away.

Place the parsnips in salted water and bring to the boil. Cook for about 5 minutes after the water comes to the boil. Drain well and cool.

Heat oil in a deep saucepan or deep fat fryer to 375°F. Fry the parsnips until golden and tender. Drain on paper towels and sprinkle lightly with salt before serving.

SERVES 4

DILLED POTATOES

New potatoes and dill are a classic combination. Here the taste of dill is used twice — dill seed to cook the potatoes and fresh dill to flavor the sauce.

─────────── INGREDIENTS ───────────

2lbs new potatoes, scrubbed □ 2 tsp dill seed □ Salt and pepper □ 4 green onions, chopped □ 1 cup natural yogurt □ 4 tbsps chopped fresh dill

Place the potatoes and dill seed into boiling salted water and cook, uncovered, for about 15 minutes or until the potatoes are just tender.

Drain the potatoes and peel off the skins. Combine the onions, yogurt and chopped dill and pour over the potatoes. Add salt and pepper and stir carefully to combine. The potatoes can be left to cool before combining with the yogurt dressing, if desired.

SERVES 6–8

ZUCCHINI RAVIGOTE

A sauce made piquant with the addition of mustard, shallots, vinegar, herbs and dill pickle. This is a classic French sauce made in a slightly different way.

─────────── INGREDIENTS ───────────

3 hard-boiled eggs □ 2 raw egg yolks □ 1 tsp Dijon mustard □ $1/3$ cup olive oil □ 2 shallots, finely chopped □ 1 dill pickle, thinly sliced □ 2 tsps chopped parsley □ 1 tsp chopped chives □ 2 tsps chopped tarragon □ 1 tbsp white wine vinegar □ Salt and pepper □ 2lbs zucchini, about 3 inches in length

Facing page: ZUCCHINI RAVIGOTE.

Place the hard-boiled egg yolks and the raw ones in a small bowl or food processor. Mix to a smooth, thick paste. Beat in the mustard and start adding the oil, drop by drop, beating constantly or with the machine running.

Add the shallots, dill pickle, herbs and vinegar, and process once or twice to mix. Shallots and pickle should still be chunky. Slice the egg whites and stir into the dressing. Taste and add seasonings. Refrigerate until ready to use.

Top and tail the zucchini and blanch in boiling salted water for about 1 minute. Drain and rinse under cold water. Pat dry and refrigerate. If small zucchini are unavailable, cut large zucchini into strips about ½ inch thick and 3 inches long.

To serve, place the zucchini in a serving dish and spoon over some of the dressing. Serve the rest of the dressing separately.

SERVES 6–8

SUNRISE SAUCE FOR VEGETABLES

This is a sauce like a thin mayonnaise with the flavor of ginger, orange and fresh tomatoes. It has a beautiful color that complements any vegetable.

INGREDIENTS

½ small onion, diced □ 3 tbsps red wine vinegar □ 2 egg yolks □ 1 cup vegetable oil □ Pinch salt and white pepper □ 1 tsp ground ginger □ Grated rind and juice of ½ an orange □ 2 tomatoes, peeled, seeded and chopped □ 2lbs baby carrots, small zucchini, green onions, small beet

Combine the onion and vinegar in a small saucepan and place over moderate heat. Cook until reduced by half.

Place the egg yolks in a food processor or blender and with the machine running, pour the oil through the funnel in a thin stream. When all the oil has been added, strain the vinegar into the mayonnaise and add salt, pepper and ginger. Process once or twice to mix.

Add the orange rind and juice and the tomatoes. Process briefly and leave at room temperature while preparing the vegetables. Peel the vegetables, if necessary and blanch in boiling water for 1–2 minutes, depending on the variety, drain and keep warm. Serve the vegetables warm with the sauce.

SERVES 6–8

PUREE
TOPINAMBOUR

Topinambour is the colorful name for a dish containing Jerusalem artichokes. These are related to sunflowers rather than globe artichokes.

─────────── INGREDIENTS ───────────

1lb Jerusalem artichokes, peeled and diced □ Pinch salt, white pepper and mace □ 1 large leek □ 4 tomatoes, peeled, seeded and quartered □ 2oz pea pods, blanched □ 2oz green beans, trimmed and blanched □ 1 small zucchini, julienned and blanched □ 4 broccoli flowerets, blanched □ 1 cup heavy cream, lightly whipped

Place the artichokes in cold water with a pinch of salt and bring to the boil in a covered saucepan. Cook until tender, then drain and purée. Add salt, pepper and mace and leave to cool completely.

Trim the leek and wash it well to remove sand and grit. Use only the white part. Separate the layers and blanch in boiling water for 2 minutes. Drain and rinse under cold water. Leave to dry. The remaining vegetables, except the tomatoes, will need about 1–2 minutes blanching. Refresh under cold water and leave to drain.

Fold the whipped cream into the artichoke purée and adjust the seasoning. Spoon into serving bowls and garnish with the vegetables.

SERVES 4

Overleaf: SUNRISE SAUCE FOR VEGETABLES.

PICKLED VEGETABLES

Combinations of crisp vegetables, spicy ginger and hot chilies preserved in jars are popular Far Eastern specialties that make 'instant' hors d'oeuvres and side dishes.

INGREDIENTS
---

1 head Chinese cabbage □ 4 green onions □ ½ cucumber □ 1 mooli radish □ 1 red chili pepper □ Fresh coriander □ 3 cloves garlic, crushed □ 4 inch piece fresh ginger, grated □ 2 tsps chili powder □ 3 tbsps sugar □ Pinch salt

---

Finely slice the Chinese cabbage. Cut the onions into 2 inch lengths. Cut the cucumber in 1 inch chunks. Slice the radish and chili pepper thinly.

Chop about 10 sprigs of coriander roughly and combine all the ingredients, stirring well. Pack the mixture into jars and pour in enough water to cover the mixture. Cover with airtight lids and leave the mixture to ferment for about 1 week.

MAKES ABOUT 4 CUPS

PARSNIP CRISPS

For crisps with a difference, try using parsnips instead of potatoes. These crisps are thick and crunchy and taste especially good with grilled meats and game.

INGREDIENTS
---

8 medium parsnips □ Oil for deep frying □ Salt

Peel the parsnips and cut them in half. Cut the thicker top half into quarters and remove the cores. Reserve the thinner ends for another use.

Facing page: PICKLED VEGETABLES.

Cut the parsnips into very thin slices and soak in cold salted water for 20 minutes. Drain and pat dry.

Heat the oil in a deep fat fryer or deep saucepan to 350°F and fry the parsnips until crisp and golden. Drain on paper towels and sprinkle lightly with salt before serving.

SERVES 4

SINGAPORE NOODLES

Pumpkin gets a completely different taste when combined with spices and Chinese noodles. If you like things spicy hot, add more cayenne or fresh chili pepper.

INGREDIENTS

$^2/_3$ cup desiccated coconut □ 2 cups boiling water □ 2 tbsps oil □ 1 clove garlic, crushed □ 1 small onion, chopped □ 1 tsp each ground cumin, coriander and turmeric □ 2lbs pumpkin, peeled, seeded and diced □ Salt and pepper □ Pinch cayenne pepper □ Juice and rind of 1 lime □ 1 tbsp cornstarch □ 8oz Chinese noodles □ ½ cup natural yogurt □ Chopped fresh coriander

Place the coconut in a bowl and pour over the boiling water. Leave to infuse for 20 minutes. Strain, pressing the coconut to extract all the liquid. Reserve coconut 'milk' and discard coconut.

Heat the oil and cook the garlic and onion until soft. Add spices and cook for 1 minute. Add the pumpkin and cook slowly for about 5 minutes. Season with salt and pepper and add cayenne and lime juice and rind. Pour on the coconut milk, cover the pan and simmer until the pumpkin is tender. Mix the cornstarch with 3 tbsps water and mix into the pumpkin.

Cook the noodles in boiling salted water until just tender. Drain and rinse under hot water. Leave to drain dry.

When the pumpkin is cooked, stir in the coriander and yogurt. Heat through, but do not boil the yogurt. Toss the sauce with noodles before serving.

SERVES 6

EGGPLANT ALEXANDRA

Puréed eggplant is often called 'caviar'. Here it combines with the real thing. To economize, substitute lumpfish caviar.

INGREDIENTS

4 eggplants □ Salt □ 3 tbsps butter □ 1 small onion, finely chopped □ White pepper □ Lemon juice □ ½ cup heavy cream, whipped □ 1 cup sour cream □ Chopped chives □ 2 tomatoes, seeded and finely diced □ 1 oz caviar

Cut the eggplants in half, score the cut surface and sprinkle with salt. Leave to stand for at least 30 minutes. The salt will draw out any bitterness in the eggplants.

Rinse the eggplants and pat dry. Wrap them in foil and cook in a moderate oven for about 40 minutes or until very soft. Scrape out the pulp carefully, preserving the skin of 1 half. Cut the skin into thin strips and reserve. Purée the pulp in a food processor.

Melt the butter in a medium saucepan and cook the onion slowly to soften. Stir in the eggplant purée and leave the mixture to cool. Season with pepper and fold in the whipped cream.

Line serving bowls with the reserved eggplant skin and spoon in the purée. Top with sour cream and sprinkle with chives. Place a spoonful of diced tomatoes in the middle and top with caviar.

SERVES 4–6

ASSIETTE DE LEGUMES

What better accompaniment to a main course could there be than a bright array of vegetables, perfectly cooked? Almost any vegetable takes well to this treatment.

1lb small new potatoes, scrubbed □ 1½lbs carrots, cut in thin strips □ 1 small head cauliflower, cut into flowerets □ 8oz green beans, trimmed □ 1 stick butter □ Salt and white pepper □ Chopped parsley and mint

Boil water in 4 medium saucepans. Start cooking the potatoes first.

After about 12–15 minutes begin cooking the rest of the vegetables until they are tender crisp and the potatoes are soft. Season with salt and pepper.

Melt the butter and toss with all the vegetables. Add the parsley to the potatoes and the mint to the carrots. Arrange all the vegetables attractively on individual side plates.

SERVES 6–8

POTATO AND MUSHROOM CROUSTADE

Packaged filo pastry leaves make this savory vegetable dish simplicity itself to prepare. With a salad to accompany it, this dish makes a wonderful light meal.

— INGREDIENTS —

10 potatoes, peeled and sliced □ 1 stick butter or margarine □ 4oz mushrooms, sliced □ 2 tbsps chopped chives □ 1lb packaged filo pastry

Bring the potatoes to the boil in salted water and precook for about 5 minutes. Drain and leave to dry out slightly.

Melt 2 tbsps butter or margarine in a frying pan and cook the mushrooms briefly. Add the chives and toss with the potatoes. Allow to cool.

Facing page: POTATO AND MUSHROOM CROUSTADE.

Unfold the sheets of pastry and place one in a 10 inch round flan dish or cake pan. Melt the remaining butter or margarine and brush the layer of pastry with some of it. Layer up five sheets of pastry, brushing each with butter or margarine. Fill with the potato mixture and cover with five more sheets of pastry, brushing each with butter or margarine.

Bake in a preheated 350°F oven until the potatoes are completely tender and the pastry is golden brown. Serve warm or cold.

SERVES 4–6

VEGETABLE GALETTE

This pastry cake is filled with parsnips and leeks in a creamy cheese sauce and is perfect for a winter's evening supper. Change the vegetables and serve it cold for summer picnics.

────────────── INGREDIENTS ──────────────

2 parsnips □ 2 tbsps butter or margarine □ 2 leeks □ 1 tbsp flour □ ½ cup milk □ Salt and pepper □ Pinch cayenne and nutmeg □ 4 tbsps cheese □ 1lb puff pastry □ 1 egg beaten with a pinch of salt

────────────────────────────────

Peel the parsnips and cut in quarters. Remove the cores and slice thinly. Place in cold salted water and bring to the boil. Cook until barely tender and then drain.

Slice the leeks thinly and wash thoroughly. Melt the butter or margarine in a saucepan and cook the leeks until tender. Remove with a draining spoon.

Stir the flour into the butter or margarine remaining in the pan, adding more if necessary. Stir in the milk gradually until smooth. Bring to the boil, whisking constantly. Add seasoning, cayenne and nutmeg, and stir in the cheese. Add the vegetables and allow to cool.

Divide the pastry in half and roll out to two circles, one 10 inches and one 12 inches in diameter. Place the smaller circle on a dampened baking sheet and brush the edge with beaten egg. Spoon on the filling to within 1 inch of the edge.

Place the larger circle on top and press the edges together to seal. Brush the top of the pastry with beaten egg and make a steam hole in the center. Score the pastry decoratively and bake in a preheated 425°F oven for 15 minutes. Lower the temperature to 375°F and cook a further 20 minutes or until pastry is risen and golden.

SERVES 6

BARLEY AND BACON PILAFF

Barley makes an interesting change from rice in a pilaff. This dish can form a tasty accompaniment to meat or poultry, or can be served on its own.

INGREDIENTS

2 cups vegetable stock □ ¾ cup pearl barley/8 strips bacon, rind and gristle removed □ 2 tbsps oil □ 1 clove garlic, crushed □ 1 head of fennel, cored and thinly sliced □ Dash Worcestershire sauce

Bring the stock to the boil in a large saucepan and add the barley. Cook until tender. Drain and keep warm.

Cut the bacon into short strips. Heat the oil in a large frying pan and add the bacon. Cook until almost crisp and add the garlic and fennel. Lower the heat and cook slowly until the fennel is tender.

Add the barley and a dash of Worcestershire sauce. Stir to mix well and heat through. Serve immediately.

SERVES 6

Chapter 8

CHEESE
SPECIALTIES

GREEN AND WHITE KEBABS

These cheese kebabs are simple but very attractive and tasty. Alter the color scheme, if desired, using black olives or cherry tomatoes as an alternative.

INGREDIENTS

4oz feta cheese □ 4oz Mozzarella cheese □ 2 large dill pickles □ 12–14 large green olives, pitted □ 3 tbsps olive oil □ 1 tbsp white wine vinegar □ Pinch sugar and cayenne pepper

Cut the cheeses into 1 inch cubes. Cut the dill pickles into thick slices or chunks and thread onto wood skewers, alternating with the 2 cheeses and the olives.

Place the kebabs on a serving plate. Mix the oil, vinegar, sugar and cayenne together and drizzle over the kebabs. Leave to marinate for about 30 minutes before serving.

SERVES 6–8

CHEESE PATCHWORK

A very eye-catching arrangement of canapés, this is also very easy to prepare and assemble. To make things even easier, it can be prepared in advance.

INGREDIENTS

12 large spinach leaves, washed □ 1 cup cream cheese □ 2 tbsps chopped mixed herbs □ 1 clove garlic, crushed □ 6 tbsps soft goat's cheese □ Lemon juice □ Coarsely ground black pepper □ 12 thin slices wholewheat bread

Facing page: GREEN AND WHITE KEBABS.

Above: CHEESE PATCHWORK.

Remove the stems from the spinach leaves and blanch the leaves in boiling water for 1 minute. Drain and refresh under cold water. Spread out on paper towels and pat dry.

Beat the cream cheese until smooth and divide in half. Add the herbs to one half and the garlic to the other. Beat the goats' cheese with black pepper and lemon juice to taste.

Spread slices of bread with the different cheese mixtures. Cover the goat's cheese spread with leaves of spinach. Cut the crusts off the bread and cut each slice into four triangles.

Arrange the cheese triangles on a serving plate. Alternate the different toppings to form a patchwork design. Prepare up to 4 hours in advance and keep covered in the refrigerator.

SERVES 10–12

GRILLED GOAT'S CHEESE

Instead of a selection of cheeses at the end of a special dinner party, try presenting just one perfectly grilled goat's cheese in a golden sesame seed coating.

INGREDIENTS
---

6 small goat's cheeses □ Oil □ Sesame seeds □ 6 slices bread, toasted □ 1 large head radicchio, washed and dried □ 1 tbsp chopped parsley

---

Brush the cheeses with oil and roll in sesame seeds to coat well.

Cut the slices of toast into rounds and place on a broiler pan.

Place a cheese on top of each and put under a moderate broiler for a few minutes or until the cheese begins to melt and the sesame seeds brown.

Place 6 of the largest radicchio leaves on serving plates and set a cheese on top of each one. Sprinkle with chopped parsley and serve immediately.

Above: GRILLED GOAT'S CHEESE.

CELERY AND WALNUT PUFFS

Choux pastry puffs make perfect cocktail savories and can be stuffed with almost any flavor filling. This one is a contrast of smooth and crunchy textures.

——————————— INGREDIENTS ———————————

¹/₃ cup water □ 2 tbsps butter or margarine, cut in small pieces □ 3 tbsps all-purpose flour □ Pinch salt □ 1 egg, beaten

——————————— FILLING ———————————

½ cup cream cheese □ 1 egg, beaten □ 1 stick celery, finely chopped □ ½ cup walnuts, chopped □ Salt and pepper □ Pinch nutmeg

Pour the water into a small saucepan and add the butter or margarine. Bring slowly to the boil. Once the butter or margarine has melted, bring to a rapid boil and then immediately remove from the heat.

Meanwhile, sift the flour with a pinch of salt onto a sheet of paper. When the water and butter mixture has boiled, tip in the flour all at once and immediately beat until the mixture leaves the sides of the pan.

Spread the mixture out onto a plate to cool completely. When cool, return it to the pan and beat in the egg. Beat vigorously until the mixture is smooth and shiny, but holds its shape.

Lightly grease a baking sheet and sprinkle it with water. Use a small spoon to drop about 18 small mounds of mixture onto the sheet.

Bake in a preheated 425°F oven for 20–25 minutes or until brown and crisp. Transfer to a wire rack to cool, and cut in half.

Beat the cheese and egg together and stir in the celery and walnuts. Add seasoning to taste and a pinch of nutmeg. Spoon some of the filling into each puff. Return to the oven for 5 minutes or until the filling is hot. Serve immediately.

MAKES 18

Facing page: CELERY AND WALNUT PUFFS.

CAVIAR AND CREAM CHEESE TARTS

Unless you splash out on real caviar, these tarts are an inexpensive yet impressive cocktail savory. They are easy to make, too, and the pastry can be frozen, baked or unbaked.

INGREDIENTS
---

2 cups wholewheat flour □ Pinch salt □ 1 stick butter or margarine □ 1 egg yolk □ Water □ 1 cup cream cheese □ $^1/_3$ cup sour cream □ 1 tbsp chopped chives □ Salt and pepper □ 2 3½oz jars of red and black caviar

---

Sift the flour with a pinch of salt into a large mixing bowl. Return the bran to the bowl. Rub in the butter or margarine until the mixture resembles fine breadcrumbs. Mix the egg yolk with about 2 tbsps cold water and stir into the flour to form a firm dough. Chill for about 20 minutes.

Above: CAVIAR AND CREAM CHEESE TARTS.

Roll out the dough on a floured surface and cut into 16 circles about 3 inches in a diameter and line tart pans or patty tins. Prick the bases and line with paper. Fill pans with beans and bake blind in a preheated 375°F oven for about 10 minutes. Remove paper and beans, and cook a further 5 minutes to crisp the bases. Remove from the pans after 5 minutes and cool on a wire rack.

Mix the cheese, sour cream and chives until smooth. Add salt and pepper to taste. Fill the tarts with the mixture, smoothing the tops. Top with red and black caviar and serve slightly chilled.

MAKES 16

ROLLED SOUFFLÉ OF LEEKS WITH PEARS AND PARMESAN

A roulade is very like a thin soufflé rolled around a flavorsome filling, in this case, ripe pears, pungent Parmesan and smooth cream cheese.

INGREDIENTS

1 stick butter or margarine ☐ 1½lbs ripe pears, peeled, cored and roughly chopped ☐ Salt and pepper ☐ Pinch nutmeg ☐ Parmesan cheese ☐ ½ cup cream cheese ☐ 1lb leeks, trimmed and washed ☐ 4 eggs, separated

Melt half the butter in a medium saucepan. Add the pears and cook, covered, over very low heat until soft. Stir frequently while cooking. Mash the pears and add seasoning and nutmeg. Allow to cool and add 3 tbsps Parmesan cheese and the cream cheese, beating the mixture well.

Slice the leeks thinly and cook in the remaining butter or margarine until soft. Purée in a food processor and mix in the egg yolks. Season with salt and pepper.

Whisk the egg whites until stiff but not dry and fold into the leek mixture. Spread the mixture into a jelly roll pan lined with non-stick baking paper. Sprinkle the top of the mixture lightly with more Parmesan cheese. Bake in a preheated 375°F oven for 10–15 minutes until risen and set.

Turn the roulade out onto wax paper or a clean towel and peel off the non-stick paper. Spread the pear filling carefully over the roulade and lift one end of the paper or towel to help roll it up. Serve immediately or reheat briefly before serving.

SERVES 6–8

HERBED CHEESE STRAWS

Cheesy pastry is always a favorite and very 'moreish' so you may want to double the recipe. The straws keep well, either airtight or frozen.

―――――――――― INGREDIENTS ――――――――――

½ cup all-purpose flour □ Pinch salt and cayenne pepper □ 3 tbsps butter or margarine □ 1 tsp finely chopped parsley, chives or dill □ 3 tbsps finely grated Cheddar

Sift the flour into a bowl or place in a food processor. Add salt and cayenne pepper, and rub in the butter or margarine. Mix in the herbs and cheese and knead lightly to bring together. Wrap the dough and chill for 20 minutes.

Roll out the dough on a floured surface to a thickness of ¼ inch. Cut into strips and twist. Place the strips on a lightly oiled baking sheet and place in a preheated 350°F oven. Bake for about 15 minutes or until pale golden brown. Transfer to a wire rack to cool.

MAKES ABOUT 30

Facing page: HERBED CHEESE STRAWS.

GRUYERE AND HAM PIE

A savory pie that can be served hot or cold is always a good recipe to have in your file. This one has the creamiest cheese filling imaginable.

INGREDIENTS
---

4 tbsps butter or margarine □ 4 tbsps flour □ 2 cups milk □ 3 cups Gruyere cheese, grated □ Salt, pepper and nutmeg □ Pinch dry mustard □ 8oz cooked sliced ham □ 1lb puff pastry

---

Melt the butter or margarine in a saucepan and stir in the flour off the heat. Whisk in the milk and return the pan to the heat. Bring to the boil, whisking constantly until thick.

Stir in the cheese and add salt, pepper, nutmeg and mustard to taste. Leave to cool completely. Press plastic wrap over the top to prevent a skin forming.

Divide the pastry in half and roll out half to line a 10 inch flan dish. Place the ham slices over the base and spoon on the cheese filling. Roll out the other half of the pastry and place on top. Seal the edges with water and bake in a preheated 375°F oven for 25–30 minutes.

Above and facing page: GRUYÈRE AND HAM PIE.

WHOLEFOOD TARTLETTES

Wholefood doesn't have to be plain or boring. These tartlettes use healthful ingredients like wholewheat flour and fresh vegetables with sophisticated flair.

--------- INGREDIENTS ---------

1 cup wholewheat flour □ Pinch salt □ 2 tbsps margarine □ 2 tbsps low fat
soft cheese □ Cold water

--------- SAUCES ---------

4 tbsps oil □ 1 large red pepper, seeded and finely chopped □ 1 tbsp
tarragon □ 2 cups natural yogurt □ 2 green onions □ 3 tbsps chopped fresh
basil □ 1 tbsp chopped parsley □ Pinch salt, pepper and sugar
□ Lemon juice

--------- FILLINGS ---------

1 small rutabaga □ 1 tbsp margarine □ 1 shallot, finely chopped □ 1 egg,
beaten □ 4 tbsps low fat soft cheese □ 1 tsp grated fresh
ginger □ Paprika □ 1 tbsp oil □ ½ tsp fennel seed □ 1 large or 2 small
zucchini, topped and tailed □ 4 tomatoes, peeled and seeded

Sift the flour into a bowl with a pinch of salt. Return the bran to the bowl. Rub in the margarine until the mixture resembles fine breadcrumbs. Use a fork to work in the soft cheese. Stir in enough water to make a firm dough.

Roll out the pastry on a floured surface. Cut into 3 inch rounds and line a muffin pan. Prick the bases of the pastry and line with wax paper. Fill with dry beans and bake in a preheated 375°F oven until browned and crisp. Remove the paper and beans and bake briefly to crisp up the bases. Allow the pastry to cool and then remove from the pan.

To prepare the sauces, heat half the oil in a small saucepan and cook the pepper slowly until softened. Add the tarragon and a few spoonfuls of water, cover the pan and cook very slowly until the pepper is soft enough to purée. Set aside to cool.

Heat the remaining oil and add the onions and herbs. Cook briefly to soften, and set aside. When the sauce mixtures have cooled completely, place one in a food processor with half the yogurt. Purée until smooth and

Above: WHOLEFOOD TARTLETTES.

add salt, pepper, sugar and lemon juice to taste. Rinse out the processor bowl and repeat with the other mixture.

Peel the rutabaga and chop it finely. Melt the margarine in a saucepan and cook the rutabaga and shallot slowly to soften without coloring. Mash and then beat in the egg, cheese and ginger. Season to taste and set aside.

Heat the oil in a separate pan and add the fennel seeds. Cook until the seeds start to pop. Grate the zucchini coarsely and add to the oil. Cook for about 2 minutes. Cut the tomatoes into thin strips and toss in the oil with the zucchini. Set aside to cool.

To serve, fill half of the tartlettes with rutabaga filling and sprinkle with paprika. Fill the other half with zucchini and tomato filling.

Cover half of each plate with the red pepper sauce and half with basil sauce. Place a rutabaga tartlette on the red pepper sauce and a zucchini and tomato tartlette on the basil sauce.

SERVES 4

Chapter 9

MEALS WITH MUSHROOMS

CHAMPIGNONS A LA BORDELAISE

This is a classic mushroom recipe. Garlic and lemon juice help to make the whole dish a most wonderful first course or accompaniment to broiled meats or poultry.

INGREDIENTS

1½lbs flat mushrooms □ 3 tbsps oil □ 2 cloves garlic, finely chopped □ 3 tbsps chopped chervil or parsley □ Juice of 1 lemon □ Salt and pepper □ Lemon slices for garnishing

---

Wipe the mushrooms and cut off the stems. Slice the caps thickly. Heat the oil in a large frying pan and add the mushrooms and garlic. Cook for about 8 minutes.

Add the chervil or parsley and lemon juice to the mushrooms. Season with salt and pepper to taste. Garnish with sliced lemon and serve immediately.

Above: CHAMPIGNONS À LA BORDELAISE.

SEAFOOD FILLED MUSHROOMS

Stuffed mushrooms are often the choice for a first course and these, with their crab meat and cream cheese filling, are especially pleasing.

--- INGREDIENTS ---

12 large mushrooms, stems removed □ 6 tbsps cream cheese □ 6 pimento-stuffed olives, finely chopped □ 1 tbsp chopped parsley □ 2oz crab meat □ ½ tsp Dijon mustard □ Salt and pepper □ Olive oil

Wipe the mushrooms with a damp cloth and place them in a baking dish.

Combine the remaining ingredients except the oil. Spoon the mixture into the mushroom caps and drizzle lightly with oil.

Bake in a preheated 350°F oven for about 10 minutes. Serve immediately.

SERVES 6

MUSHROOM AND WATERCRESS ROULADE

A light, savory roulade is an excellent appetizer. This delicious version also makes an interesting and tasty vegetarian main course.

--- INGREDIENTS ---

4 tbsps butter or margarine □ 1lb mushrooms finely chopped □ Salt and pepper □ 4 eggs, separated □ Small bunch watercress □ 1 cup fromage frais □ Lemon juice □ 1 tbsp chopped parsley

Melt the butter in a frying pan and add the chopped mushrooms. Cook quickly to drive off moisture. Season and mix with the egg yolks.

Whisk the egg whites until stiff and fold into the mushroom mixture. Line a jelly roll pan with non-stick paper and lightly oil the paper. Spoon in the mixture and spread evenly. Bake in a preheated 375°F oven for 15 minutes.

Pick over the watercress and discard any thick stalks and roots. Chop the leaves finely.

Turn out the roulade onto a clean towel and scatter over the watercress. Roll up and keep warm.

Mix fromage frais with lemon juice to taste and the parsley. Season with salt and pepper. Slice the roulade to serve and spoon over some of the sauce.

MARINATED MUSHROOMS

Mushroom lovers will adore this simply prepared appetizer, salad or side dish. It looks attractive spooned into radicchio leaves to serve as an easy first course.

INGREDIENTS

1lb mushrooms □ 1 shallot, finely chopped □ ½ cup olive oil □ 4 tbsps white wine vinegar □ 1 tsp crushed coriander seeds □ Salt and pepper □ 1 red or yellow pepper, seeded and thinly sliced □ Chopped parsley □ Coriander leaves

Wipe the mushrooms and leave whole if small or quarter them if large. Combine in a bowl with the shallot.

Mix the oil, vinegar, coriander seeds and seasonings and pour over the mushrooms. Stir to coat evenly and refrigerate for about 2 hours.

To serve, garnish with pepper slices and sprinkle with chopped parsley. Add the coriander leaves and serve cold.

Facing page: MARINATED MUSHROOMS.

MUSHROOM TRIO ON TAGLIATELLE

This is fast food with style. Mushroom lovers will adore this dish, which combines three varieties of their favorite ingredient.

―――――――――――――― INGREDIENTS ――――――――――――――

2oz dried Italian or Chinese mushrooms, soaked in hot water. □ 12oz tagliatelle □ 2 tbsps butter □ 1 shallot, finely chopped □ 1 clove garlic, crushed □ 3oz button mushrooms, sliced □ 12oz canned Chinese straw mushrooms, drained □ 1 cup heavy cream □ Salt and pepper □ 4 black olives, pitted and chopped

When the mushrooms have softened, drain them and remove the tough stems. Slice the caps thinly and set aside.

Cook the pasta in boiling salted water until al dente. Rinse under hot water and drain.

Melt the butter in a medium saucepan and cook the shallot and garlic to soften but not brown. Add the button mushrooms and cook 2 minutes. Add the dried mushrooms and straw mushrooms and pour on the cream.

Bring the mixture to the boil and cook until the cream thickens slightly. Season with salt and pepper and pour over the pasta. Sprinkle with the chopped olives to serve.

SERVES 4

MUSHROOMS IN A LOAF

For a sophisticated snack, try these little loaves filled with a rich and creamy mushroom mixture with a hint of sherry.

Facing page: MUSHROOM TRIO ON TAGLIATELLE.

INGREDIENTS
---

18 mushrooms ☐ ⅓ cup butter or margarine ☐ 4 tbsps sherry ☐ ½ cup
heavy cream ☐ Pinch nutmeg ☐ Salt and pepper ☐ 6 bread rolls,
white or wholewheat

Slice the mushrooms thinly. Melt the butter or margarine in a saucepan
and cook the mushrooms for a few minutes. Add the sherry and bring to
the boil. Cook to evaporate the alcohol.

Add the cream and bring back to the boil to reduce it slightly. Add a
pinch of nutmeg and seasoning.

Take a thin slice off the top of each roll and scoop out the insides,
leaving a border of bread. Heat the rolls in a hot oven for 1–2 minutes. Fill
with the mushroom mixture and place on the tops. Serve immediately.

SERVES 6

MUSHROOMS PROVENÇALE

*This dish perks up plainly cooked meat or poultry and is even delicious with fish and
seafood. It's equally good as a light main course with a salad.*

INGREDIENTS
---

2 tbsps olive oil ☐ 24 flat mushrooms ☐ Salt and pepper ☐ 1lb canned
tomatoes ☐ 1 tbsp chopped parsley ☐ 2 tsps chopped fresh thyme ☐ 1 clove
garlic, crushed ☐ 2 tsps tomato paste ☐ Pinch sugar ☐ 6 black olives, pitted

---

Heat the oil in a saute pan and briefly cook the mushrooms. Sprinkle with
salt and pepper, transfer to a serving dish, and keep warm.

Add the tomatoes to the pan, breaking them up with a fork. Add the
herbs, garlic and tomato paste. Season and add a pinch of sugar. Bring the
sauce to a rapid boil and cook quickly to reduce the quantity and
concentrate the flavors. Pour over the mushrooms and garnish with black
olives.

SERVES 6

MUSHROOM FRITTERS

If you love mushrooms you won't be able to resist these. Perhaps it would be wise to double or triple the recipe!

———————————— INGREDIENTS ————————————

36 even-sized mushrooms □ Seasoned flour □ 1–2 eggs, beaten □ Fresh breadcrumbs □ Oil for deep frying □ Salt □ 1 cup mayonnaise □ 1 clove garlic, crushed □ Dash tabasco □ Lemon wedges

Wipe the mushrooms with a damp cloth, but do not submerge them in water. Roll them in the seasoned flour, and then dip into the beaten eggs, coating completely.

Roll in the breadcrumbs and set aside. Heat the oil to 375°F and fry about 6 at a time until crisp on the outside, but still firm inside. Drain on paper towels and sprinkle lightly with salt.

Mix the mayonnaise with the garlic and tabasco and spoon into individual dishes. Place the mushrooms on serving plates and garnish with lemon wedges. Serve with the garlic mayonnaise for dipping.

SERVES 6

STUFFED MUSHROOMS

Among the most versatile appetizers in any cookbook are mushrooms stuffed with a savory filling. This recipe is low in calories as well as high on flavor.

———————————— INGREDIENTS ————————————

6 large, flat mushrooms □ 1 green pepper, seeded and finely diced □ 1 cup cottage cheese □ 1 clove garlic, crushed □ 2 tsps fresh basil □ 1 tbsp freshly grated Parmesan cheese □ Salt and pepper □ 1 cup grated Cheddar □ 1 small egg □ Paprika

Remove the mushrooms stems and chop them finely. Peel the mushrooms, if necessary, and place them in a shallow baking dish.

Mix the mushroom stems with the green pepper, cottage cheese, garlic, basil, Parmesan, salt and pepper. Spoon the filling on top of each mushroom cap.

Combine the Cheddar with the egg and mash to a paste. Spoon some on top of each stuffed mushroom and spread out carefully. Sprinkle with paprika and bake in a moderate oven for 10 minutes. Place under a preheated broiler for a few minutes to brown, and serve immediately.

SERVES 6

CHAMPIGNONS FARCIS D'EPINARD

Stuffed mushrooms are ever popular as a first course and can make a lovely vegetarian main course, too.

INGREDIENTS

2lbs fresh spinach, washed □ 4 tbsps butter □ 2 green onions, finely chopped □ Salt and pepper □ Pinch nutmeg and dry mustard □ 24 flat mushrooms □ ¾ cup finely grated cheese □ 2 egg yolks □ Black olives □ Chopped parsley

---

Cook the spinach in only the water that clings to the leaves after washing. When just wilted, remove from the pan and press dry. Chop finely.

Heat 1 tbsp of butter and add the onions. Cook a few seconds and then add the chopped spinach. Cook quickly to evaporate any excess moisture in the spinach. Add seasoning to taste and the nutmeg and mustard.

Wipe the mushrooms and reserve 4. Trim the stems from the remaining mushrooms and chop them finely, leaving the caps whole. Melt the remaining butter in a frying pan. Place in the mushroom caps and cook briefly. Remove the caps and add the chopped stems. Cook briskly until all moisture evaporates. Combine the cooked stems with the spinach.

Above: CHAMPIGNONS FARCIS D'EPINARD.

Add half the cheese to the mixture and beat in the egg yolks. Place the mushroom caps rounded side down in a baking dish. Fill the caps with the spinach mixture and sprinkle with the remaining cheese. Bake in a preheated 325°F oven for about 15 minutes. Brown under a preheated broiler, if desired.

Slice the 4 reserved mushrooms and toss the olives in the chopped parsley. Place stuffed mushrooms on serving plates and garnish with sliced mushrooms and olives.

SERVES 6

Chapter 10
ENTERTAINING DISHES

CHEESE DIAMONDS

Easy-to-make cocktail or after dinner savories are always a welcome entertaining idea. You wouldn't expect anything that tastes so good to be so simple to fix.

—————— INGREDIENTS ——————

8oz puff pastry □ 1 beaten egg □ 1 cup blue cheese, crumbled □ ½ cup cream cheese □ 1 stick celery, finely diced □ Cream □ Dash tabasco

Roll out the pastry to a rectangle about ⅛ inch thick. Cut into diamond shapes and score the tops of half of the diamonds.

Place on baking sheets and brush the tops with beaten egg. Bake in a preheated 425°F oven for 15 minutes until risen and brown. Cool on a wire rack.

Beat the cheeses together and add the celery and enough cream to make a mixture that can be piped. Add tabasco and pipe the mixture onto the bottom halves of the diamonds. Place on the tops and serve.

SPINACH AND WATERCRESS SOUP

This rich soup, with its dark green color, can be served hot or cold, so it's perfect for either winter or summer.

—————— INGREDIENTS ——————

4 tbsps butter or margarine □ ½ small onion, finely chopped □ 2 potatoes, peeled and sliced □ 5 cups stock □ 4oz fresh spinach, well washed □ 2 bunches watercress, well washed □ Salt and pepper □ Pinch nutmeg □ 1 cup heavy cream

Previous pages: STUFFED ONION GRATINÉE, PORT AND STILTON POTS, EXTRA SPECIAL MINCE PIES, CRANBERRY RHUBARB SPARKLE, and ARTICHOKE CREAMS. **Facing page:** CHEESE DIAMONDS.

Melt the butter in a large saucepan and cook the onion slowly to soften. Add the potatoes and pour on the stock. Bring to the boil then simmer slowly until the potatoes are tender.

Add the spinach to the pan. Pick over the watercress and discard any discolored leaves, thick stems and roots. Add to the pan and cook for a few minutes.

Pour into a food processor and purée until smooth. Process in 2 or 3 batches. Add salt, pepper and nutmeg. Return the soup to the rinsed out pan and add the cream. Bring to the boil and then simmer to cook and thicken the cream. If serving cold, chill at least 4 hours or overnight.

SERVES 6–8

EGGPLANT CAVIAR

Inexpensive, despite the name, this is a sophisticated cocktail savory with as much style and taste as the real thing.

INGREDIENTS

1 eggplant □ 3 tbsps oil □ 1 clove garlic, crushed □ 1 shallot, finely chopped □ 1 tbsp tomato paste □ 1 tsp lemon juice □ Pinch salt and pepper □ Rye bread, cut in small squares □ Large dill pickle, sliced □ Flat parsley or coriander leaves

Cut the eggplant in half and lightly score the cut surfaces. Sprinkle with salt and leave to stand 30 minutes. Rinse well and pat dry. Wrap in foil and bake in a moderate oven for about 30 minutes, or until very soft.

Heat the oil in a saucepan and cook the garlic and shallot to soften. Stir in the tomato paste, lemon juice and seasonings.

Cut the eggplant into small pieces and place in a food processor with the saucepan ingredients. Process until coarsely chopped. To serve, mound on top of squares of rye bread and garnish with sliced dill pickle and parsley or coriander leaves.

SERVES 4–6

Facing page: EGGPLANT CAVIAR.

ARTICHOKE CREAMS

Artichoke leaves make an attractive and edible garnish surrounding smooth and creamy mousses made with artichoke hearts. This is a sophisticated appetizer for that special dinner party.

INGREDIENTS
---

2 globe artichokes □ ½ cup light stock or white wine □ 1½ tbsps gelatin □ 14oz canned artichoke hearts, drained □ 4 eggs, separated □ 1 cup milk □ Pinch ground mace and ground rosemary □ Salt and white pepper □ 1 cup whipping cream □ ½ cup oil □ 3 tbsps lemon juice □ Pinch sugar

---

Cut the stems off the base of each artichoke and trim off the tips of the leaves. Place in a large saucepan of boiling water and cook for about 40 minutes, or until bottom leaves pull off easily.

While the artichokes cook, soak the gelatin in the stock or wine in a small saucepan.

When the artichokes are done, remove them from the pan and drain upside down. Allow to cool. Pull off all the leaves and reserve them. Scrape away the thistle-like choke and discard it.

Cut the artichoke bottoms into small pieces and combine in a food processor with the canned artichoke hearts. Purée until smooth.

Beat the egg yolks until thick and lemon-colored. Scald the milk and whisk it gradually into the egg yolks. Strain the mixture back into a saucepan and place over low heat. Cook, stirring constantly, until the mixture coats the back of a spoon. Stir in the gelatin, ground mace and rosemary and seasonings. Combine with the artichokes and purée again until well mixed.

Place the mixture in the refrigerator until thickened but not completely set. Check and stir the mixture often. Whisk the egg whites until stiff but not dry and whisk the cream until soft. Fold both into the cooled artichoke mixture.

Facing page: ARTICHOKE CREAMS.

Lightly oil 8 small molds and spoon in the mixture. Leave in the refrigerator to set completely. Turn out onto plates to serve.

Mix the remaining ingredients together well to make the dressing. Surround each artichoke cream with some of the reserved artichoke leaves and pour over some of the dressing.

SERVES 8

CURRIED POTATO SOUP

Curry powder adds a golden color and interesting taste to potatoes in this easy to make, warming and delicious soup.

INGREDIENTS
---

4 tbsps butter or margarine □ 1 small onion, finely chopped □ 1 clove garlic, crushed □ 1 tbsp mild curry powder □ 1 tsp ground coriander □ 1lb potatoes, peeled and sliced □ 4 cups chicken or vegetable stock □ Salt and pepper □ ½ cup natural yogurt □ Milk □ Chopped chives □ Croutons (optional)

Melt the butter or margarine in a large saucepan and cook the onion and garlic slowly until soft but not colored. Add the curry powder and coriander and cook for 1 minute.

Add the potatoes and pour on the stock. Cover and cook slowly until the potatoes are very soft. Purée the mixture in a food processor in 2 batches. Return to the pan and reheat. If the soup is very thin, boil rapidly, stirring frequently, until thickened. Season to taste.

Mix the yogurt with enough milk to bring it to the consistency of light cream. Drizzle the yoghurt over the soup and top with chopped chives. Serve with croutons, if desired.

SERVES 4–6

Facing page: CURRIED POTATO SOUP.

EIGHT-TREASURE PANCAKES

Eight is a very good number in Chinese tradition. There are eight major ingredients in this recipe rolled up in the lightest and most delicate of pancakes.

--------- INGREDIENTS ---------

1 cup rice flour □ ¾ cup water □ Pinch salt □ 8 dried mushrooms, soaked □ Oil □ 1 clove garlic, crushed □ 4oz chicken breast, skinned and boned □ 2 carrots, peeled and finely shredded □ 1 large green pepper, seeded and finely shredded □ 6oz bean sprouts, washed □ 2 green onions, shredded □ 3 inch piece fresh ginger, peeled and finely shredded □ 4oz cooked crabmeat □ ¾ cup finely shredded almonds □ Sesame seed oil □ Sherry □ Soy sauce □ Sugar

Place the rice flour in a bowl or food processor. Mix in the water until the batter is smooth. Add a pinch of salt and leave the batter to stand while preparing all the filling ingredients.

Set all the filling ingredients aside to cook later. Lightly oil a frying pan and place over high heat. When the pan starts to smoke, spoon in small amounts of batter and spread into small, thin discs. Cook on both sides until lightly browned. Repeat until all the batter is used. Set the pancakes aside and keep warm.

Drain the mushrooms and remove the stalks, slice the caps finely and set them aside.

Heat the oil in a wok or large frying pan and add the garlic. Cook a few minutes to flavor the oil and then remove and discard the garlic. Shred the chicken finely and stir-fry in the oil until tender, then set it aside.

Cook the mushrooms, carrots, green pepper, bean sprouts, onions and ginger separately for a few minutes. The vegetables should still be crisp. Place them in separate serving dishes as they are cooked.

Add the crabmeat to the oil in the pan and stir fry for a few seconds. Remove to a serving dish and add the almonds to the pan. Cook, stirring constantly, until pale brown.

Facing page: EIGHT TREASURE PANCAKES.

Drain the oil from the wok or pan and add about 3 tbsps sherry and soy sauce per person. Add 2 tsps sugar per person and a few drops sesame seed oil. Bring the mixture to the boil and then simmer about 2 minutes or until the alcohol from the sherry evaporates. Pour into small dishes to use for dipping.

To serve, place the pancakes on a serving dish and arrange the separate dishes of filling ingredients around them. Give each person a bowl of dipping sauce and let everyone assemble their pancakes with a choice of fillings.

SERVES 6–8

TERRINE OF SMOKED FISH

Smoked fish is always a favorite for appetizers. This pretty, stripy terrine looks special enough for any dinner party or buffet table.

INGREDIENTS

4 tbsps dry white wine □ 4 tsps gelatin □ 6oz smoked salmon □ 1 large smoked mackerel fillet □ 1lb smoked cod roe □ Pinch cayenne pepper □ Juice and grated rind of 1 lemon □ 2 egg whites □ 1 cup heavy cream □ Salt and pepper □ Oil □ 2 tbsps chopped parsley □ 2 tbsps chopped chives □ 1 lemon, sliced, for garnishing

Pour wine into a small saucepan. Sprinkle over the gelatin and leave to soak.

Cut smoked salmon into thin strips. Skin mackerel and cut into thin slivers.

Cut the cod roe in half and scoop out the center into a bowl. Mix in up to 4 tbsps hot water to make a smooth paste. Mix in the cayenne pepper, lemon juice and rind.

Dissolve gelatin over gentle heat and stir gradually into the roe. Whisk the egg whites until stiff but not dry and whisk the cream until soft peaks form. Fold both into the roe mixture. Taste and adjust the seasoning.

Lightly oil a 2 pint terrine or loaf pan. Spoon $1/3$ of the roe mixture into the terrine or pan. Layer on half of the smoked salmon and mackerel and sprinkle with half of the chopped herbs.

Cover with another $1/3$ of the roe mixture. Repeat the smoked fish and herb layer, covering with the remaining $1/3$ of the roe mixture.

Make sure the mixture is well packed down. Cover with oiled foil and press down gently. Chill at least 4 hours, preferably overnight.

To unmold, loosen the sides of the mixture carefully with a knife and dip the base of the terrine or pan briefly into hot water. Invert onto a serving plate and shake the mold sharply to loosen. Garnish with twists of lemon and sprinkle the top with more chopped chives and parsley, if desired.

SERVES 10–12

PASTRY SLICES WITH LEEK AND EGG FILLING

INGREDIENTS

8oz puff pastry □ 8 quail's eggs, hard-boiled □ 2 leeks, halved and washed □ 1 stick butter □ 4oz oyster mushrooms □ $1/2$ cup brown stock □ $1/3$ cup dry white wine □ Salt and pepper □ 2 tomatoes, peeled, seeded and diced □ Chives, cut in 1 inch pieces

Roll out the pastry about $1/4$ inch thick and cut out 4 ovals. Place them on a dampened baking sheet and bake in a preheated 425°F oven until crisp and risen. Keep warm.

Peel the quail's eggs and leave in cold water.

Blanch the leeks in boiling salted water for 1–2 minutes or until just tender. Drain and pat dry with paper towels. Keep warm.

Melt 1 tbsp butter in a pan and briefly cook the mushrooms. Season and keep warm.

Bring the stock and wine to a rapid boil in a saucepan and reduce by half. Gradually beat in the remaining butter, off the heat, until the sauce thickens.

Cut the pastry ovals in half and place the bottoms on serving plates. Slice the eggs and arrange on the pastry. Top with the leeks and spoon over some of the sauce. Place on the pastry tops. Pour remaining sauce around the pastry and garnish with the mushrooms. Sprinkle the diced tomato over the mushrooms and add the chives.

SERVES 4

SAVORY LEEK AND HAM ROLL

Roly poly pudding was never like this! This savory version makes a perfect appetizer or a light supper. While it must cook for several hours, it's worth the wait.

─────────── INGREDIENTS ───────────

──────── FILLING ────────

8oz ham, chopped ☐ 2 large leeks, washed and chopped ☐ 2 tsps chopped thyme ☐ 1 tbsps chopped parsley ☐ Salt and pepper

──────── PASTRY ────────

1½ cups flour ☐ 1 tsp baking powder ☐ ⅓ cup suet ☐ Water

Prepare all the filling ingredients and combine them.

Sift the flour and baking powder into a bowl with a pinch of salt. Stir in the suet and enough water to make a light, soft dough.

Roll out the dough on a floured surface to a rectangle about ¼-inch thick. Scatter the filling ingredients over the surface and roll up like a jelly roll.

Wrap the roll in buttered foil, sealing tightly but leaving room for the dough to rise. Wrap in a clean towel and tie both ends.

───────────────────────

Facing page: SAVORY LEEK AND HAM ROLL.

Place on a rack above simmering water in a roasting pan that has a lid. Steam for about 2 hours, checking the water level frequently.

Unwrap the roll and place on a baking sheet. Place in a preheated 375°F oven for about 10 minutes or until browned slightly. Serve immediately.

STUFFED ONIONS GRATINEE

An unusual dish for a main course or appetizer, this can be prepared in advance so it's great for holiday meals or weekends.

INGREDIENTS

4 large onions □ 2 tbsps butter or margarine □ 8oz turkey breast fillets, finely diced □ 8oz gammon, finely diced □ 1 tsp chopped sage □ 1 tsp thyme □ 2 tbsps chopped parsley □ ½ cup brown breadcrumbs □ 2 eggs, slightly beaten □ 1 cup heavy cream □ 1 cup freshly grated Parmesan cheese □ Pinch salt, pepper and nutmeg □ Paprika

Peel the onions and blanch in boiling water. Cut them in half around the middle. Trim off the root hairs. Carefully cut out the middle of the onions and chop finely. Leave 2 of the outer layers together to form 'shells'.

Melt the butter or margarine in a medium saucepan and cook the chopped onions until softened. Add the turkey to the pan to partially cook it.

Stir in the gammon, herbs, breadcrumbs, salt and pepper. Stir in enough of the eggs to bind the mixture together. Spoon the filling into the onion 'shells' and place them in a shallow oven-proof dish.

Boil the cream to reduce and thicken it. Stir in half the cheese and add nutmeg, salt and pepper to taste. Spoon the sauce over the onions and sprinkle the top with the remaining cheese.

Bake in a preheated 400°F oven for 25 minutes, or until bubbling. Brown under a preheated broiler before serving, if desired.

Facing page: STUFFED ONIONS GRATINÉE.

TABBOULEH

This is a Middle Eastern specialty. The wheat grains are very good for your health and they taste good, too.

───────────────── INGREDIENTS ─────────────────

½ cup bulgur wheat □ 1 tbsp chopped coriander □ 2 tbsp chopped parsley □ 2 tbsps lemon juice □ ⅓ cup olive oil □ Pinch salt and pepper □ 1 large tomato, cored and chopped

───

Soak the bulgur wheat in cold water to cover for about 1 hour until the grains expand and absorb most of the water. Drain well and spread out onto a clean towel to dry. Fluff up occasionally to keep the grains separate.

Place the grains in a salad bowl and add the herbs, lemon juice, on and seasonings. Toss with the tomatoes and serve.

VEGETABLES IN

A PASTRY PAN

For fun, create a serving dish out of filo pastry to hold your vegetables. The pastry can be bought ready made in most supermarkets, so this is easy, too.

───────────────── INGREDIENTS ─────────────────

16 sheets filo pastry □ 1½ sticks butter or margarine, melted □ 1½lbs of assorted vegetables such as: □ Green beans, trimmed □ Cauliflower flowerets □ Baby carrots, peeled □ Turnips, peeled and sliced □ Broccoli flowerets □ Pea pods, trimmed □ Cherry tomatoes, peeled □ Button mushrooms, quartered. □ Salt and pepper □ Lemon juice

───

Unfold the pastry sheets. Reserve 4 tbsps butter for adding to the vegetables. Use some of the remaining butter to lightly grease a large

───

Facing page: VEGETABLES IN A PASTRY PAN.

frying pan with an ovenproof handle. Line the base of the pan with a pastry sheet. Brush it with butter and cover with another pastry sheet. Repeat with 10 more sheets to use 12 in all.

Press the pastry to mold it to the shape of the pan and trim the edges. Butter the remaining 4 sheets and stack them. Roll them up to form a handle for the pan. Stick the pastry handle to the pastry base and extend it 6 inches up the real pan handle. Bake in the preheated 400°F oven until brown and crisp.

Meanwhile prepare the vegetables and blanch them in boiling salted water until tender crisp. If using mushrooms cook them in melted butter for about 3 minutes. Cook cherry tomatoes for 1 minute in butter.

To serve, toss all the vegetables in butter and add lemon juice and seasoning. Keep them warm. Carefully detach the cooked pastry pan from the real pan and place it on a large serving plate. Fill with the hot vegetables and serve immediately.

SERVES 6

Salade Extraordinaire

This salad really is extraordinary. It requires a lot of work, but the end result is well worth the effort.

INGREDIENTS

5lb duck □ Oil □ Salt □ ¾ cup hazelnuts □ ½ cup hazelnut oil □ 1 tbsp tarragon vinegar □ Freshly ground black pepper □ Pinch sugar and dry mustard □ 1lb fresh spinach, well washed □ 2 tbsps butter □ 1 clove garlic, crushed □ Pinch nutmeg □ 1 egg, beaten □ 1 cup heavy cream □ 12 raw oysters, shelled □ ½ cup dry white wine □ ½ cup fish or vegetable stock □ 1 bay leaf and blade mace □ 1 tbsp lemon juice □ Frisee (curly endive) □ 1 tomato, peeled, seeded and sliced

Facing page: SALADE EXTRAORDINAIRE.

Prick the duck skin all over with a fork. Rub the skin lightly with oil and sprinkle with salt. Place the duck on a rack in a roasting pan. Roast in a preheated 425°F oven for 25 minutes. Remove the duck breasts and continue roasting the legs for a further 25 minutes.

Skin the duck breast and cut the meat in julienne strips. Return the skin to the oven with the duck legs. Pour off the fat from the roasting pan occasionally during cooking.

At the same time the duck is cooking, brown the hazelnuts on a baking sheet. Stir them occasionally for even browning. Allow to cool and crush roughly.

When the duck legs are cooked, remove them from the oven and allow the duck to cool. If the skin is not crisp, remove the leg skin and return to the oven with the breast skin, raise the oven temperature to 450°F and cook until the skin is crisp enough to crumble. Drain the crumbled skin on paper towels and reserve.

When the duck cools, bone the legs and cut the meat into small dice. Combine it with the hazelnuts. Combine the oil, vinegar, black pepper, sugar and mustard, and mix with the duck and hazelnuts. Refrigerate until needed.

Remove the stems and center rib from 12 large unblemished spinach leaves and blanch in boiling water. Remove after 1 minute. Drain on paper towels and reserve. Add the remaining spinach to the water and cook for about 3 minutes.

Drain well and squeeze out any excess moisture. Melt the butter in a saucepan and cook the spinach, garlic and nutmeg over high heat to drive out all remaining liquid.

Purée in a food processor and add the egg, cream and seasoning. Place a spoonful of the mixture on each reserved spinach leaf and fold up the sides to form a parcel. Refrigerate until needed.

Place the oysters, wine, stock, bay leaf and blade mace in a saucepan. Bring the liquid to simmering and cook 1 minute. Remove the oysters from the pan. Bring the liquid to the boil and cook rapidly to reduce by half. Strain into a clean pan. Add the cream to the strained liquid and re-boil a few minutes to thicken the cream. Season and add the lemon juice. Allow to cool.

To assemble, add the reserved crumbled duck skin to the leg meat and hazelnuts in the dressing. Spoon an equal portion onto serving dishes. Scatter over the julienned duck breast. Place 2 spinach parcels and 2 oysters on each plate and spoon the cream sauce over the oysters. Garnish with frisee and tomato.

SERVES 6

GELEE CASSIS

Blackcurrants with creme de cassis make a flavorful and very French jellied dessert. Since it's made with canned blackcurrants, you can enjoy it anytime of year.

INGREDIENTS

2lbs canned blackcurrants in natural juice □ 1 cup sugar □ 2 tbsps
gelatin □ ⅓ cup water □ ½ cup creme de cassis

Strain the currants and combine the juice with the sugar. Push the fruit through a strainer and stir the purée into the sugar and juice.

Soak the gelatin in the water and dissolve over gentle heat. Add the cassis to the blackcurrant purée and measure. Make up to 2 pints with water if necessary. Stir in the dissolved gelatin.

Pour the mixture into a dampened 2 pint mold and chill until set.

SERVES 8

Above: GELÉE CASSIS.

EXTRA SPECIAL MINCE PIES

The time and effort spent on these very festive pies will be amply repaid in compliments and praise. And after all, Christmas comes but once a year!

INGREDIENTS

2 cups all-purpose flour □ 1½ sticks butter or margarine □ 2 tsps sugar □ 1 egg yolk □ 4 tbsps ice cold water □ Few drops almond extract □ 8oz prepared mincemeat □ 3 tbsps brandy or sherry □ Fine granulated sugar □ Glace chestnuts □ 4 cups powdered sugar □ 1 tsp mixed spice □ Sliced almonds

To prepare the pastry, sift the flour into a large bowl or process once or twice in a food processor. Rub or process in the butter or margarine until the mixture resembles fine breadcrumbs.

Stir in the sugar and combine the egg yolk and water with the almond extract. Add to the flour and fat and mix to a firm dough. Cover the pastry and chill it for about 20 minutes.

Roll out ⅔ of the pastry to a rectangle about ⅛ inch thick. Cut into 3 inch rounds with a fluted pastry cutter. Line 16–20 tart pans with the pastry.

Mix the mincemeat with the brandy or sherry and fill each tart about ¾ full with the mixture.

Combine the trimmings with the remaining ⅓ of the pastry and roll out again slightly thinner. Use a 2½ inch fluted pastry cutter to cut several rounds. Use these to cover the tops of some of the pies completely. Cut a steam hole in the top of each of these pies.

Use a 1 inch fluted pastry cutter to cut several smaller rounds of pastry. Use a star shaped cutter to cut several pastry stars. Bake the circles and stars on a baking sheet in a preheated 400°F oven along with the pies for about 20 minutes. Place the pastry shapes on the lowest shelf in the oven.

To finish, sprinkle the tops of the covered pies with fine granulated sugar while slightly warm. Place the small circles on some of the open pies and top with chestnuts. Allow the stars to cool completely and

Facing page: EXTRA SPECIAL MINCE PIES.

sprinkle with powdered sugar. Place the stars on some of the open pies.

Sift the powdered sugar with the mixed spice and add enough water to make a thick icing. Spoon some on the remaining open pies and top with sliced almonds.

MAKES 16–20 PIES

PORT AND STILTON POTS

For a savory at a festive holiday meal, this mixture of cheese and port is hard to surpass. It keeps well, too, thanks to the clarified butter seal on top.

INGREDIENTS

1lb Stilton □ 1 stick unsalted butter □ ¹/₃ cup port □ ¹/₃ cup chopped walnuts □ 1 stick salted butter □ Bayleaves

Mix the Stilton and unsalted butter to purée in a food processor or with an electric mixer. Mix ¹/₃ of the purée with the port. Add the walnuts to the other ²/₃ of the mixture.

Marble the 2 mixtures together, taking care not to over mix. Pack into a deep dish or terrine. If desired, make individual pots.

Melt the salted butter in a small saucepan and bring to the boil. Take off the heat and allow to settle. Skim the salt off the top, pour off the buttery oil and reserve it. Discard the sediment or save it to mix with hot vegetables.

Spoon the clarified butter over the top of the cheese. Once the butter sets, garnish with bayleaves.

SERVES 10–12

Facing page: PORT AND STILTON POTS.

MOKA MOLD

The rich taste of coffee is a surprising flavor for a jelly, but a pleasing one. Set in a decorative mold this makes a very elegant dinner party dessert.

――――――― INGREDIENTS ―――――――

2 cups strong, black coffee □ ½ cup sugar □ ½ cup water □ 1 tbsp gelatin □ 1 cup heavy cream □ 3 tbsps coffee liqueur □ Coffee bean chocolates to decorate

Make the coffee and leave to cool slightly. Combine the sugar with half the water and bring slowly to the boil to make a syrup. Combine with the coffee.

Dissolve the gelatin in the remaining water and stir into the coffee syrup. Strain through a fine sieve and cool completely.

Pour into a dampened 3 cup ring mold and refrigerate until set. To serve, lightly whip the cream and fold in the liqueur. Turn out the mold and fill the center with the cream. Decorate with the chocolate coffee beans.

Above: MOKA MOULD.

WINE AND CITRUS PYRAMID

Packet gelatine dessert makes this spectacular mold spectacularly easy. Try it even if you don't have a pyramid mold — it looks lovely set in just a glass bowl.

--------- INGREDIENTS ---------

1 packet lime gelatine dessert ☐ 1 packet orange gelatine dessert ☐ 1 bottle dry white wine

Follow the package directions to dissolve the gelatines. Use hot water as the package suggests and add white wine to make up to the full quantity of liquid. Make each gelatine in a separate bowl.

Pour a layer of one flavor into a dampened 4 cup mold and chill until set. Pour on another flavor and chill again until that layer is set. Repeat with remaining gelatines.

Refrigerate until completely set before turning out to serve.

CRANBERRY RHUBARB SPARKLE

A cool, sparkling jelly makes exactly the right ending to a rich meal. A blend of rhubarb and cranberries tastes especially fresh and light.

--------- INGREDIENTS ---------

8oz cranberries ☐ ½ cup water ☐ 1 cup sugar ☐ 1 stick cinnamon ☐ 12oz rhubarb, fresh, canned or frozen, cut into 1 inch pieces ☐ 3 tbsps water or lemon juice ☐ 1½ tbsps gelatin

Pick over the cranberries and discard any that are damaged or discolored. Place the berries in a heavy-based saucepan with the water and cinnamon. Place the pan over gentle heat and bring slowly to simmering.

When the berries have softened, but are still whole, stir in the sugar. Bring to a rolling boil and then remove from the heat. Take out half of the berries to use as a decoration.

If using canned rhubarb, drain thoroughly and combine with the remaining cranberries and juice. If using fresh or frozen rhubarb, cook with the cranberries and juice until the rhubarb is soft. Reserve a few whole pieces of rhubarb to use as a decoration, if desired.

Remove the cinnamon stick and purée the remaining rhubarb with the cranberries and juice in a food processor and then push through a sieve to make the mixture smoother.

Sprinkle the gelatin on top of the water or lemon juice in a small saucepan and allow to soak. Dissolve over gentle heat, pour into the purée and stir well. Dampen 6 small molds with water and pour in the purée. Chill in the refrigerator until set. When set, turn out onto dessert plates and top with the reserved cranberries and pieces of rhubarb.

BOMBE DE LA SAINTE-MARIE

Looking as if it would take hours to make, this ice cream dessert really couldn't be easier. Fresh flowers provide a colorful, spring-like look.

--- INGREDIENTS ---

2 cups vanilla ice cream □ 4 tbsps ground almonds □ 8oz fresh raspberries □ Sugar □ ½ cup lemon curd □ Fresh fruit and flowers to decorate

Place ice cream in a bowl and beat in the ground almonds. Pack the mixture into 6 small molds and freeze until firm.

Purée the raspberries and sieve to remove the seeds. Add sugar to taste and a little water if the sauce is too thick.

Beat the lemon curd to thin it down slightly. Spoon a thin layer on each dessert plate. Dip the molds very briefly in hot water and invert onto the lemon curd. Spoon raspberry sauce on top of the ice cream and decorate with fruit and flowers.

Facing page: CRANBERRY RHUBARB SPARKLE.

MARBLED PEACHES AND CREAM

Set in an intricate mold, this dessert looks like cool, carved marble. The look belies its smooth, velvety texture and creamy taste.

INGREDIENTS

8 ripe peaches, peeled and sliced ☐ 3 tbsps lemon juice ☐ 2 tbsps gelatin ☐ ¾ cup cream cheese ☐ ⅓ cup sugar ☐ 1 cup whipping cream ☐ Vanilla extract

Purée the peaches in a food processor. Soak half the gelatin in the lemon juice and then dissolve over gentle heat. Pour into the peaches and blend thoroughly.

Combine the remaining gelatin with 3 tbsps water and leave to soak. Beat the cream cheese until soft. Dissolve the gelatin over low heat and stir gradually into the cream cheese. Whip the cream and fold into the cheese mixture.

Chill both mixtures until nearly set and then fold together to marble. Pour into a lightly oiled 2 pint mold and chill until completely set before turning out.

Facing page: MARBLED PEACHES AND CREAM.
Above: BOMBE DE LA SAINTE-MARIE.

Above: Zucchini Nut Loaf, Raisin Nut Bread,
Wholewheat Fruit Bread, **and** Rich Egg Bread.

WHOLEWHEAT FRUIT BREAD

This healthy wholewheat loaf is packed with fruit. Cherries and pineapple are used here,
but you can make the recipe your own by using your favorite choices.

INGREDIENTS

$^{1}/_{3}$ cup + 1 tbsp milk □ 1½ tbsps yeast □ 1 tsp sugar □ 2 eggs, beaten □ 3
cups wholewheat flour □ Pinch salt □ 4 tbsps butter, softened □ 8oz canned
cherries, drained and pitted □ 4oz canned pineapple chunks, drained
□ 1 tsp honey

Heat the milk to a hand-hot temperature. Stir in the yeast and sugar. Leave in a warm place for about 10 minutes, or until frothy. Stir in the eggs.

Sift the flour and a pinch of salt into a bowl and make a well in the center. Return the bran to the bowl. Pour the yeast mixture into the well and beat with a wooden spoon to gradually incorporate the flour. Beat for about 10 minutes.

Cream the softened butter into the dough and beat to mix well. Cover the bowl and leave the dough in a warm place to rise for about 40 minutes.

When the dough has almost doubled in bulk, beat in the prepared fruit and the honey. Turn immediately into a lightly oiled loaf pan. Cover and allow to rise a second time for about 10–15 minutes.

Bake in a preheated 400°F oven for about 50 minutes. Allow to cool in the pan for a few minutes, then loosen the sides and turn out to cool on a wire rack before slicing to serve.

MAKES 1 LOAF

ZUCCHINI NUT LOAF

This tea bread is spicy, nutty and it doesn't taste like zucchini! These breads, which depend on baking powder to help them rise, don't require kneading so are easy to make.

───────── INGREDIENTS ─────────
2 cups all-purpose flour ☐ 2 tsps baking powder ☐ 1 tsp ground
ginger ☐ Pinch salt ☐ ¾ cup sugar ☐ 2 small eggs ☐ ¹/₃ cup oil ☐ 1 cup
roughly chopped almonds ☐ 6oz zucchini, sliced

Sift the flour, baking powder, ginger and salt into a mixing bowl. Add the sugar and make a well in the middle of the ingredients.

Place the eggs and oil in the well and beat with a wooden spoon, gradually incorporating the dry ingredients. Stir in the almonds and zucchini until well mixed.

Spoon into an oiled 1lb loaf pan lined with wax paper and smooth the top. Place in a preheated 350°F oven and bake for about 1 hour on the middle rack. A skewer inserted into the middle of the loaf will come out clean when the bread is done.

Allow the loaf to cool in the pan for about 30 minutes. Loosen from the sides of the pan and use the paper to help remove the bread. Cool on a wire rack before slicing to serve.

MAKES 1 LOAF

RAISIN NUT BREAD

A loaf of freshly baked bread is one of the nicest things in the world to eat, especially when it's filled with raisins, nuts and spice.

INGREDIENTS

4 tbsps warm water □ 1 tbsp yeast □ ½ tsp sugar □ 1 cup milk □ 1½ tbsps butter or margarine □ 4 cups white bread flour □ 2 tbsps light brown sugar □ Pinch salt □ 1 tsp cinnamon □ 1 cup chopped walnuts □ 1 cup raisins

Heat the water to a hand-hot temperature and stir in the yeast and sugar. Leave in a warm place for about 10 minutes, or until frothy.

Heat the milk and butter gently until the butter melts and the milk is hand-hot. Combine with the yeast mixture.

Sift the flour into a large bowl and stir in the sugar, salt and cinnamon. Make a well in the center and pour in the yeast and milk mixture. Mix with a wooden spoon, gradually incorporating the dry ingredients.

Turn the dough out onto a floured surface and knead for about 10 minutes, or until smooth and elastic. Place in an oiled bowl and cover. Set in a warm place for about 1 hour, or until doubled in bulk.

Punch the dough down, turn out and knead in the chopped nuts and the raisins. Shape into a loaf and fit into a 1lb pan. Cover and leave to rise a second time until the dough comes to the top of the pan.

Bake in a preheated 400°F oven for about 45 minutes, or until the top is golden brown and the bottom sounds hollow when tapped. If the loaf is not done after 45 minutes, remove it from the pan, turn it upside down and bake a further 5 minutes. Allow to cool on a wire rack.

RICH EGG BREAD

This rich dough with a good pinch of herbs makes wonderful sandwiches and delicious toast.
For use serving sweet toppings, just omit the herbs from the dough.

INGREDIENTS

½ cup milk □ 1½ tbsps yeast □ 2 tbsps sugar □ 4 eggs □ 5 cups all-purpose
flour □ Pinch salt □ 1 stick + 2 tbsps butter, softened □ 2 tbsps chopped fresh
herbs □ 1 egg, beaten with a pinch of salt

Heat the milk to a hand-hot temperature. Stir in the yeast and sugar and
leave in a warm place for about 10 minutes, or until frothy. Beat in the
eggs.

Sift the flour with a pinch of salt into a large bowl and make a well in
the center. Pour the yeast mixture into the well and beat to gradually
incorporate the dry ingredients.

Beat in the softened butter until completely incorporated. Turn out
onto a floured surface and divide in half. Knead the chopped herbs into
half of the dough until smooth and elastic. Place in an oiled bowl and
cover.

Fruit, nuts, herbs and vegetables make delicious bread
ingredients.

Knead the plain dough and place in a separate covered bowl. Leave the doughs in a warm place to rise for about 1 hour, or until almost doubled in bulk.

Punch down both doughs and knead again briefly. Shape into loaves and place each in an oiled 1lb loaf pan. Cover and leave to rise a second time.

Brush the top of each loaf with egg glaze and bake in a preheated 400°F oven for 30–40 minutes, or until the tops are golden brown and the bottoms sound hollow when tapped.

Cool briefly in the pans and then loosen the sides carefully. Turn the loaves out onto a wire rack to cool before slicing to serve.

PINEAPPLE FLING

A lovely cocktail with the taste of the tropics and the surprise addition of Drambuie.

INGREDIENTS

Ice cubes □ 6 measures pineapple juice □ 2 measures coconut liqueur □ 2 measures Drambuie □ 2 twists of lime peel □ 2 fresh flowers

Place the ice cubes in each glass and pour over pineapple juice, coconut liqueur and Drambuie. Stir and decorate the glasses with lime peel and fresh flowers.

KIR ECOSSAIS

A French drink – white wine and crème de cassis – takes a trip to Scotland and adds Drambuie to its list of ingredients.

INGREDIENTS

1 cup dry white wine □ 2 measures Drambuie □ 2 measures crème de cassis □ 2 large strawberries □ 2 clusters red currants with leaves

Facing page: PINEAPPLE FLING.

Pour chilled white wine into each glass. Add 1 measure of Drambuie and 1 of crème de cassis to each. Stir and decorate the glass with the fruit.

SERVES 2

ORANGE MAGIC

A frothy orange creation, this cocktail has a blue layer of Curacao that appears like magic when it's stirred.

———————————————— INGREDIENTS ————————————————

4 measures Grand Marnier ☐ 4 measures orange juice ☐ 2 egg whites
☐ 2 tsps powdered sugar ☐ Ice cubes ☐ 2 tsps blue Curacao

Place the Grand Marnier, orange juice, egg whites and sugar in a cocktail shaker. Add the ice cubes, cover and shake until very frothy.

Strain into chilled cocktail glasses. Spoon the Curacao into each glass and swirl through the foam until a blue layer forms. Serve immediately.

SERVES 2

HIGHLAND MIST

Creme de menthe gives this cocktail its minty color and flavor and a dash of fresh spring water gives it sparkle.

———————————————— INGREDIENTS ————————————————

Ice cubes ☐ 4 measures Drambuie ☐ 1 measure vodka ☐ 4 measures creme
de menthe ☐ Carbonated mineral water ☐ Fresh flowers

Place ice cubes in each glass. Pour over 2 measures of Drambuie and ½ of vodka. Add 2 measures of creme de menthe and fill the glasses with carbonated mineral water. Decorate with flowers.

SERVES 2

Facing page: ORANGE MAGIC.

APRICOT SUNSHINE

A sunny apricot-colored cocktail, this is slightly sweet, with the crisp cool taste of cucumber to offset the sweetness.

─────────────── INGREDIENTS ───────────────

Crushed ice □ 2 measures apricot nectar □ 2 measures vodka □ 2 measures Strega □ 2 apricot halves □ 2 thin slices cucumber □ 2 cocktail cherries □ 2 mint leaves

───

Place crushed ice in 2 cocktail glasses. Mix together the nectar, Strega and vodka and pour over the ice. Thread an apricot half and cucumber slice on a cocktail stick and add cherries. Place on the glasses to decorate. Add mint leaves.

SERVES 2

SPICED WHITE WINE

When the weather gets cold and the season gets festive, a warming and equally festive beverage is called for. This is a light, fragrant change from mulled red wine.

─────────────── INGREDIENTS ───────────────

1 oz cube sugar □ 1 orange □ ½ cup brandy □ Rind of 1 lemon, pith removed □ 1 lemon, orange or apple stuck with cloves □ Bay leaves or stick cinnamon □ 1 bottle dry white wine

───

Flavor and color the sugar cubes by rubbing them over the orange. Place the sugar in a punch bowl and pour over the brandy.

Add the remaining ingredients, except the wine and leave to stand for about 1 hour.

To serve, heat the wine gently until almost boiling. Pour the wine over the ingredients in the punch bowl and stir well. Serve immediately.

MAKES 8–10 CUPS

Facing page: APRICOT SUNSHINE.

Chapter 11

FRUIT FANTASIES

Spirited Apple and Blackberry Mold

INGREDIENTS

1½lbs blackberries □ 1½lbs apples □ ⅓ cup sugar □ 1½ tbsps gelatin □ 4 tbsps water □ 4 tbsps Calvados or brandy

Place the blackberries in a heavy-based pan. Peel, core and slice the apples and add to the pan. Bring slowly to the boil and then add the sugar. Simmer until the fruit is soft.

Soak the gelatin in the water in a small pan. Dissolve over gentle heat. Purée the fruit and then strain to remove the seeds. Push as much of the purée as possible through the sieve. Stir in the gelatin and the Calvados or brandy and pour the mixture into a 3 cup mold and chill until set.

SERVES 6

St. Clement's Jelly

A jelly is the lightest of puddings. This one is made even lighter because it's whipped into a froth of fine bubbles. The orange and lemon flavor is as cool as can be.

INGREDIENTS

Juice and rind of 2 small lemons □ ⅓ cup fine granulated sugar □ 1 cup water □ 2 tbsps gelatin □ 2 cups orange juice □ Orange or lemon slice for decoration

Previous pages: FRAISES D'AMOUR. Facing page: SPIRITED APPLE AND BLACKBERRY MOLD.

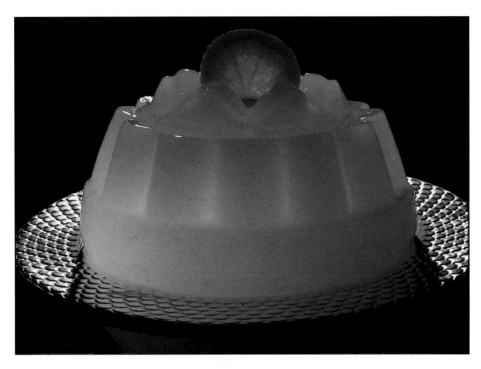

Above: St. Clement's Jelly.

Combine the lemon rind, sugar and half the water in a saucepan and place over low heat. Cook slowly until the sugar dissolves. Leave to infuse for about 30 minutes.

Soak the gelatin in the remaining water for about 5 minutes and then dissolve over gentle heat and pour into the sugar syrup.

Add the lemon juice and orange juice to the syrup and stir to blend all the ingredients and dissolve the gelatin. Allow to cool completely and then refrigerate until half set.

Whisk by hand or with an electric mixer until full of very fine bubbles. Pour into a dampened 3½ cup mold and chill until set. Turn out and decorate as desired.

FRUIT AND FLOWER SALAD

Fresh fruit and flowers make a delicious combination in this pretty summer dessert. Cardamoms lend a lovely fragrance and flavor to the lemony syrup.

INGREDIENTS

¾ cup sugar ◻ 1 cup water ◻ Juice of 2 small lemons ◻ 4 oranges, peeled and
segmented ◻ 1 small pineapple, peeled, cored and cubed ◻ 2 pears, peeled,
cored and sliced ◻ 2 apples, peeled, cored and sliced ◻ 2 bananas, peeled and
sliced ◻ 4oz seedless green grapes ◻ 4oz black grapes, seeded ◻ 12 green
cardamom pods ◻ ⅓ cup Cointreau ◻ Small fresh flowers

Combine the sugar and water in a heavy-based saucepan and bring slowly
to the boil. When the sugar has dissolved, boil rapidly until clear and
syrupy. Take off the heat and add the lemon juice. Leave to cool
completely.

Add the oranges and remaining fruit to the syrup, stirring to coat all
the pieces. Crush 4 cardamom pods and add to the fruit along with the
whole pods. Add the Cointreau and mix well. Chill for at least 1 hour in
the refrigerator. Garnish each serving with fresh flowers.

SERVES 6

MELON AND BLUEBERRY SPARKLE

*This is a refreshing appetizer or dessert that is very pretty, too. Pink- or green-fleshed melons
are both equally attractive and when blueberries are not available, substitute fresh or canned
blackcurrants.*

INGREDIENTS

6oz blueberries ◻ Sugar ◻ 2 tbsps water ◻ 3 melons
◻ Champagne or sparkling white wine

Wash the blueberries and remove any stems. Place in a saucepan with
sugar to taste. Add the water and cook slowly until the berries burst and
juices become syrupy. Sieve, pushing as much pulp through as possible.
Chill the purée in the refrigerator.

Cut the melons in half and scoop out the seeds. Place a spoonful of
the purée in each melon. Fill with champagne or sparkling wine. Serve
immediately.

POEME DE FRUITS

The recipe names translates as 'poem of fruit'. It is truly a masterpiece of elegant and delicious composition.

--------- INGREDIENTS ---------

¾ cup sugar ☐ 1½ cups water ☐ 8 greengages or plums ☐ 4 tbsps lemon juice ☐ 1 tbsp gelatin ☐ 1 cup heavy cream ☐ 1 tbsp plum brandy ☐ 2 cups red wine ☐ ¾ cup sugar ☐ 1½lb blackcurrants ☐ 1 stick cinnamon ☐ 6 ripe dessert pears ☐ 4oz each of 3 different sorbets ☐ Mint leaves to garnish

Combine the sugar and water in a saucepan and bring slowly to the boil. Swirl the pan occasionally to help dissolve the sugar evenly. Allow the syrup to boil for about 5 minutes to thicken slightly.

Above: POEME DE FRUITS.

Cut the greengages or plums in half and remove the stones. Place the fruit in the syrup and poach gently until soft. Meanwhile, sprinkle the gelatin over the lemon juice in a small saucepan.

When the fruit is soft, remove it from the syrup. Chop 2 halves roughly and set them aside. Purée the rest. Heat the gelatin gently to dissolve, and combine it with the fruit purée in a bowl. Leave to cool.

Reserve 6 tbsps of the cream to use as decoration and whip the rest until soft peaks form. Stir in the plum brandy. When the fruit purée has completely cooled, fold in the whipped cream and the chopped fruit. Pour the mixture into 6 lightly oiled molds. Chill about 2 hours or until set.

Combine the red wine and sugar in a saucepan large enough to hold six pears. Bring slowly to the boil, swirling the pan occasionally to help the sugar dissolve evenly. Add the blackcurrants and cook slowly until tender. Remove half the blackcurrants to use as a decoration and purée the remainder with the wine syrup. Sieve to remove the seeds.

Return the syrup to the saucepan and add the cinnamon stick. Peel the pears and remove the 'eyes' on the bottom of each. Leave the stems on and place the pears upright in the syrup. Bring slowly to the boil and simmer until tender. Cooking time will vary according to the ripeness of the pears. Leave the pears to cool in the liquid. Remove the cinnamon stick.

To serve, spoon the blackcurrant sauce from the pears onto each serving plate. Place a pear on each plate. Loosen the greengage or plum molds and turn one out onto each plate. Place 1 scoop of each different flavor sorbet on the plates and add the reserved blackcurrants. Drizzle the reserved cream around the edge of the sauce and use a knife or skewer to make a pattern on each plate. Decorate with the mint leaves and serve immediately.

SERVES 6

FRAISES D'AMOUR

Strawberries in a creamy custard set in a heart shape make a delightful dessert for a Valentine's Day dinner or any special meal.

INGREDIENTS

1 tbsp gelatin □ 4 tbsps eau de fraises or Cointreau □ 5 egg yolks □ ½ cup sugar □ ½ cup milk □ 1 cup heavy cream □ 1lb strawberries, washed and hulled

Combine the gelatin and liqueur in a small saucepan and leave to soak.

Whisk the egg yolks and the sugar together until thick and mousse-like. Scald the milk and whisk it into the egg and sugar mixture. Strain into a heavy-based saucepan and place over low heat. Stir continuously until the mixture thickens and coats the back of a spoon. Allow to cool completely.

Dissolve the gelatin over gentle heat and pour into the cooled custard. Place over ice and stir until beginning to set. Take off the ice, whip the cream lightly and fold into the custard.

Slice the strawberries, leaving a few whole to use as decoration, if desired. Arrange a pattern of strawberries in the bottom of an oiled heart-shaped mold. Place strawberries against the sides of the mold and pour in a layer of custard. Fold the remaining strawberries into the rest of the custard and pour into the mold. Chill until set.

To serve, dip the mold briefly into hot water and invert a large serving dish over the top. Turn the mold and dish over and shake sharply to release the custard. Decorate the top with the reserved strawberries.

SERVES 8

GLACE DE NOIX DE COCO SENEGAL

Coconut ice cream, made the easy way, combines with exotic fruit in this tropical fantasy.

———————————— INGREDIENTS ————————————

1 pint natural vanilla ice cream □ Half a fresh coconut, grated □ 1 mango □ 1 lime □ Pinch sugar □ 4 fresh figs □ 4 mint leaves □ Fresh seasonal fruit □ Green food coloring

Combine the ice cream with the coconut, reserving 4 tbsps of the coconut for decoration. Scoop into 4 mounds and flatten the tops slightly. Place on a baking sheet and freeze until firm.

Facing page: GLACE DE NOIX DE COCO SENEGAL.

Peel the mango and cut the flesh away from the stone. Purée the fruit with a juice of the lime and a pinch of sugar, if needed. Let down the sauce with a small amount of water.

Remove the peels from the figs except for the stem ends. Cut off the stems and make small slits to insert the mint leaves.

Place the reserved coconut in a jar with a few drops of green food coloring. Cover the jar and shake it vigorously to tint the coconut. Remove the ice cream from the freezer and roll the sides of each ball in the tinted coconut.

Pour the mango sauce onto dessert plates and put one ball of ice cream in the middle of each one. Top with a fig. Arrange fruit around the ice cream and serve immediately.

SCARLET FRUIT SALAD

A fruit salad can be as elegant a dessert as any pastry, as this recipe so beautifully illustrates. As it's so much lower in calories, too, you can have just that little bit extra!

―――――――――――――― INGREDIENTS ――――――――――――――

1lb raspberries □ Powdered sugar □ Lemon juice □ 2 tbsps raspberry liqueur □ 3 tbsps cream □ 3 figs □ 8oz alpine strawberries □ 8oz redcurrants

Place half of the raspberries in a food processor and purée until smooth. Taste and add sugar and lemon juice as necessary. Sieve to remove the seeds. Add the raspberry liqueur and, if the sauce is too thick, let down with a little water.

Mix 3 tbsps of the sauce with the cream and set aside. Quarter the figs and remove stems from the strawberries and currants.

Coat the bases of 6 dessert plates with the raspberry sauce and pour the raspberry cream sauce around the edge. Arrange the remaining raspberries, figs, strawberries and currants on top of the sauce, and use a skewer to swirl the two sauces together in an attractive pattern.

Facing page: SCARLET FRUIT SALAD.

Chapter 12

INDULGENT DESSERTS

PINEAPPLE COCONUT ROLL

The tropical taste of coconut and pineapple is a heavenly combination. Add a smooth custard and the lightest of cakes and the result is divine.

INGREDIENTS

4 eggs □ ½ cup sugar □ ¾ cup all-purpose flour □ 1 tsp baking powder □ 1
cup cream □ 3 tbsps desiccated coconut □ 3 eggs, beaten □ 2 tbsps
sugar □ 1 tbsp cornstarch □ 1 small pineapple, peeled, cored and
chopped □ ½ cup whipping cream □ 2 tbsps coconut liqueur
(optional) □ Toasted desiccated coconut

Place the eggs and sugar in a large bowl. Beat until the mixture is thick and mousse-like. Sift in the flour and baking powder and fold into the egg and sugar mixture. Spread the mixture into a 14 × 9 inch jelly roll pan lined with lightly oiled non-stick baking paper. Bake in a preheated 375°F oven for about 12 minutes, or until the top springs back when touched lightly.

Meanwhile, scald the cream with the coconut and leave to infuse. Beat the eggs, sugar and cornstarch together and pour on the cream. Place over low heat and stir constantly until the mixture thickens. Place wax paper on the surface of the filling and allow it to cool.

Turn the cake out onto a clean towel and peel off the paper. Reserve half the pineapple and chop the rest very finely. Stir into the filling and spread over the surface of the warm cake. Lift the edge of the towel and roll up the cake around the filling. Allow to cool completely and then chill in the refrigerator.

Whip the cream and fold in the coconut liqueur. Pipe or spoon over the top of the roll and decorate with the reserved pineapple pieces. Sprinkle with toasted coconut to serve.

SERVES 8

Previous page: OEUFS À LA NEIGE EN PYRAMIDE.
Facing page: PINEAPPLE COCONUT ROLL.

SPICED CARROT AND NUT CAKE

A rich, spicy cake, this is nevertheless good for you thanks to a healthy proportion of carrots in the mixture.

INGREDIENTS

2 cups all-purpose flour □ 2 tsp baking powder □ 2 tsps mixed spice □ 1½ cups granulated brown sugar □ Pinch salt □ 1 cup vegetable oil □ 4 eggs, beaten □ 12oz carrots, peeled and grated □ 4oz chopped almonds

FILLING

1 stick butter □ 1 cup cream cheese □ 4 tbsps powdered sugar □ 1 tsp vanilla extract

Grease three 8-inch cake pans and place a circle of wax paper in the bottom of each. Lightly grease the paper and dredge the inside of the pans with flour. Tap out the excess.

Above: SPICED CARROT AND NUT CAKE.

Sift the flour, baking powder and spice into a bowl. Add the sugar and a pinch of salt and make a well in the center. Pour the oil and eggs into the well and add the carrots and almonds. Stir the mixture until all the ingredients are well mixed.

Divide the mixture between the pans and smooth the tops. Place the pans in a preheated 375°F oven for about 40 minutes. Change the position of the pans after about 20 minutes. When the cakes are done, the center will spring back when lightly touched. Allow to cool in the pans for a few minutes and then transfer to a wire rack to cool.

Beat the butter and cream cheese together to soften. Gradually beat in the powdered sugar and add the vanilla. Beat until light and fluffy.

Sandwich the layers together with the cream cheese filling. The top may be sprinkled with powdered sugar, if desired.

SERVES 8

MINCEMEAT ROULADE

After Christmas, when you've had your fill of mince pies, but don't know what to do with that bit of left over filling, try folding it into a light and fluffy roulade for a delicious change.

—————————— INGREDIENTS ——————————

4 eggs, separated □ ½ cup sugar □ 8oz bottled mincemeat □ 4 tbsps flour, sifted □ ½ tsp baking powder □ ½ cup heavy cream □ Powdered sugar □ 2 tbsps rum

Beat yolks and sugar until thick and mousse-like. Beat the whites until stiff but not dry and fold into the yolks with the mincemeat and sifted flour.

Spread into a 12 × 8 inch jelly roll pan lined with non-stick baking paper. Bake 10–15 minutes in a preheated 375°F oven.

Cool on a wire rack and then cover with a damp cloth. Leave several hours or overnight.

Above: MINCEMEAT ROULADE.

Turn out onto wax paper sprinkled with powdered sugar. Lightly whip the cream and add sugar to taste. Stir in the rum and spread over the roulade. Roll up, using the paper to lift the end of the roulade, and sprinkle with more powdered sugar to serve.

GRANITE AU VIN ROUGE

This wine ice with its crisp, crunchy texture and refreshing taste, is a perfect ending for a rich meal. It also looks beautiful in a dessert glass.

INGREDIENTS

½ cup granulated sugar □ 1 cup water □ Peel of 1 orange □ Juice of ½ a lemon □ 2 allspice berries □ 1 bottle red wine

Combine the sugar, water, orange peel, lemon juice and allspice berries in a heavy-based saucepan. Bring slowly to the boil, swirling the pan occasionally to help the syrup dissolve evenly. Boil for about 5 minutes to thicken slightly and strain.

Return the syrup to the pan and add the wine. Bring back to the boil and simmer for a few minutes. Allow the mixture to cool completely. Pour into a shallow container and freeze until almost solid. Alternatively, use an ice cream freezer according to the manufacturer's directions, although the texture will be slightly different.

Break up the ice crystals several times until the mixture is completely frozen. Allow to freeze until solid. If the mixture doesn't freeze, add more lemon juice or water. Break up into small chunks and spoon into glasses to serve.

SERVES 6

Above: Granite au Vin Rouge.

CHERRY CHOCOLATE CORDIAL WITH ICE CREAM

Ingredients needn't be exotic to make an inviting dessert. Cherries, chocolate and ice cream are all readily available, and combined they make an irresistible treat.

INGREDIENTS

1 pint natural vanilla ice cream ☐ 2lbs fresh cherries ☐ 4 squares semi-sweet chocolate ☐ 4 tbsps Cherry Heering liqueur

Use an ice cream scoop to make 1 or 2 mounds of ice cream per person. Place on a baking tray and freeze.

Pit all the cherries and leave the stems attached to 40 of the best looking ones. Chop the other cherries roughly and place in a pan with enough water to cover. Cook slowly until very tender. Purée in a food processor and then sieve, if desired. Return the sauce to the rinsed out pan and add the cherries with stems. Poach about 5 minutes or until just tender.

Remove the cherries from the saucepan and add the chocolate, chopped in small pieces. Heat slowly to melt the chocolate. Remove from the heat and add water if the sauce is very thick. Stir in the Cherry Heering liqueur.

Pour the sauce onto 4 dessert plates and place on 1 or 2 scoops of ice cream. Surround the ice cream with the whole cherries and serve immediately.

SERVES 4

Facing page: CHERRY CHOCOLATE CORDIAL WITH ICE CREAM.

CHOCOLATE MOUSSE CAKE

This super-rich dessert is like chocolate velvet. For all it's impressive looks and fantastic taste, it's very easy to make.

──────────── INGREDIENTS ────────────

15–20 lady fingers □ 3 eggs, separated □ 4 tbsps sugar □ 4 squares semi-sweet chocolate □ 4 squares unsweetened chocolate □ 2 tbsps coffee or orange liqueur

Use the fingers to line a 2 pint loaf pan. Whisk the egg yolks and sugar until thick and mousse-like.

Melt the 2 chocolates with the liqueur and allow to cool slightly. Stir into the yolks and sugar.

Whisk the egg whites until stiff, and fold into the chocolate mixture. Pour into the loaf pan and refrigerate until completely set. Turn out and slice to serve.

OEUFS A LA NEIGE EN PYRAMIDE

Sometimes called snow eggs and sometimes floating islands, these tender meringues poached in milk are tender and light. A crisp almond topping makes a delicious contrast.

──────────── INGREDIENTS ────────────

6 eggs, separated □ 1½ cups fine granulated sugar □ Grated rind of 1 orange □ 2½ cups of milk

──────────── CARAMEL ALMOND TOPPING────────────

½ cup granulated sugar □ ¹/3 cup water □ ½ cup sliced almonds □ Few drops almond extract

Beat the egg whites until stiff but not dry. Gradually beat in 1 cup of the fine granulated sugar, beating well in between each addition.

Bring the milk to simmering in a large frying pan. Use two spoons to shape the meringue mixture into ovals and drop them into the milk. Cook about 20 seconds or until beginning to puff. Turn over and cook the other side for about 10 seconds. Set the meringue ovals aside to cool.

Beat the egg yolks with the fine granulated sugar and the orange rind. Pour on the milk used to cook the meringues. Pour into a saucepan and cook over low heat, stirring continuously until the mixture thickens and coats the back of a spoon. Strain into a large serving bowl and chill. When cold, pile the meringues on top.

To prepare the caramel almond topping, place the granulated sugar and water in a small, heavy-based pan. Heat slowly until the sugar dissolves. Turn up the heat and boil rapidly, swirling the pan occasionally. Cook until the syrup turns golden brown. Take off the heat immediately and add the almond extract.

Sprinkle the almonds over the meringues and quickly pour over the syrup, allowing it to drip down the sides. Let the caramel set before serving.

SERVES 6

SUGAR GLAZED FRUIT AND CREAM

Seasonal fruit covered in whipped cream is treated to a caramelized sugar glaze for a spectacular dessert that is extremely easy to make.

—————————————— INGREDIENTS ——————————————

2 bananas, sliced □ 2 ripe pears, peeled, cored and sliced □ Lemon juice □ 4 oranges, peeled and segmented □ Small bunch white and black grapes □ 1½ cups heavy cream □ ¾ cup sugar □ ⅓ cup water

Toss the banana and pear slices in lemon juice to prevent discoloration. Place in a large glass bowl with the oranges and grapes. Pit the grapes, if necessary.

Whip the cream until stiff and spoon in mounds on top of the fruit. Refrigerate until well chilled.

Combine the sugar and water in a heavy-based saucepan and heat slowly to dissolve the sugar. Bring to the boil and cook rapidly until golden brown.

Dip the base of the pan in cold water to stop the cooking, and drizzle over the cream. Allow the caramel to harden completely before serving.

SERVES 4

PRALINE COOKIE CAKE

This cake has very intriguing striped layers of cake, buttery almond cookies and smooth butter cream. On top, crisp praline provides a sparkly finish.

--------- INGREDIENTS ---------
¾ cup unblanched almonds □ ⅓ cup sugar
--------- CAKE LAYER ---------
4 eggs □ ½ cup sugar □ ¾ cup flour □ 4 tbsps butter, melted
--------- COOKIE LAYER ---------
1lb amaretti cookies □ ⅓ cup butter, melted
--------- FILLING ---------
2 egg whites □ 1 cup powdered sugar □ 1 stick unsalted butter
□ 2 tsps Amaretto

Combine the almonds and sugar in a heavy-based pan and place over low heat until the sugar dissolves. Turn up the heat and cook until the sugar caramelizes and the almonds begin to pop. Pour out onto an oiled baking sheet and leave to harden. Once cool, grind in a food processor.

Whisk the egg and the sugar together until thick and mousse-like. Sift the flour and fold into the mixture. Drizzle the butter over the top and fold in. Spoon the cake batter into a greased and floured 8 inch square pan. Bake in a preheated 375°F oven for about 20 minutes or until the mixture pulls away from the sides of the pan and the top springs back when lightly touched. Cool on a wire rack.

Previous pages: Sugar Glazed Fruit and Cream.
Above: Praline Cookie Cake.

Crush the amaretti cookies in a food processor and blend in the butter. Press the mixture onto non-stick paper into 3 thin 8-inch squares. Chill until firm.

To prepare the butter cream, whisk the egg whites and sugar in a bowl over simmering water until very thick and holding peaks. Soften the butter and beat the meringue mixture in bit by bit. Add the Amaretto.

To assemble the cake, invert one of the cookie layers onto a serving plate and peel off the paper. Spread with some of the butter cream. Cut the cake into 3 thin layers and place one on the butter cream. Top with another cookie layer and continue sandwiching the cake and cookie layers together, reserving enough butter cream for the outside. If the cookie layers should break, just press them back together or sprinkle over the icing.

Spread the butter cream on the top and sides of the layers and coat completely with the praline. Refrigerate for about 20 minutes to firm up the icing and cut in slices to serve.

SERVES 8–10

HAZELNUT APRICOT MERINGUE CAKE

Light layers of meringue combine with toasted hazelnuts, apricots and lots of whipped cream to make a perfectly heavenly cake.

───────────── INGREDIENTS ─────────────

6 egg whites □ 1½ cups fine granulated sugar □ 2 cups toasted, chopped hazelnuts □ 3 cups heavy cream □ 4 tbsps apricot brandy □ 7oz canned apricots, drained □ Sugar □ Candied apricots to decorate

Whisk the egg whites until stiff but not dry. Gradually whisk in the sugar, making sure the egg whites are stiff again after each addition. When the meringue is stiff and glossy, fold in half the toasted hazelnuts.

Line 2 baking sheets with non-stick baking paper and spread half of the mixture on each in a 10 inch circle. Bake in a preheated 275°F oven for about 1¼ hours or until pale brown and crisp. Turn upside down on wire cooling racks and peel off the paper. Leave to cool completely.

Whip the cream and add the apricot brandy. Remove about ¹/₃ of the cream and add the canned apricots, chopped in small pieces. Add sugar to taste, and about 4 tbsps of the remaining hazelnuts. Sandwich and meringue layers together with the apricot filling.

Cover the top and sides of the cake with the remaining cream and sprinkle with the remaining hazelnuts. Chop the candied apricots into small pieces with a hot knife and use to decorate the top of the cake. Refrigerate for about 1 hour before serving.

SERVES 10

Facing page: HAZELNUT APRICOT MERINGUE CAKE.

BAVARIAN APPLE CAKE

Pumpernickel bread, with its rich brown color and nutty flavor, is used instead of flour in this recipe, making it almost more a bread pudding than a cake.

─────────────── INGREDIENTS ───────────────

3 large cooking apples □ ½ cup packed soft brown sugar □ ¹/₃ cup water □ 4 tbsps butter or margarine □ 2 tbsps brandy □ Grated rind and juice of 1 lemon □ ½ cup ground hazelnuts □ ¼ cup golden raisins □ 4 cups pumpernickel bread, crumbled □ 2 eggs, separated □ 2 dessert apples, peeled, cored and thickly sliced □ 14oz canned apricot halves □ 1 stick cinnamon □ 2 tsps cornstarch □ Oil

Place the cooking apples in a heavy-based saucepan with the sugar and water. Cook slowly until soft but not falling apart. Stir in the butter or margarine, brandy, lemon rind, hazelnuts, golden raisins, and pumpernickel crumbs.

Beat the egg yolks until thick and fold into the apple mixture. Whisk the egg whites until stiff but not dry and fold in until well incorporated.

Lightly oil a deep cake pan and line the bottom with wax paper. Spoon in the cake mixture and bake in a preheated 350°F oven for about 1 hour, or until a skewer inserted into the center of the cake comes out clean.

Meanwhile, cook the dessert apple slices in enough water to cover and add some of the lemon juice. When the apples are tender, take off the heat and leave in the liquid.

Place the apricots and their juice in a saucepan with the cinnamon stick. Cook slowly until very soft. If the liquid evaporates, add some of the cooking liquid from the sliced apples. When the apricots are soft, remove the cinnamon and purée them in a food processor.

Combine the cornstarch with the remaining lemon juice and mix with the apricot purée. Pour into a saucepan and bring slowly to the boil, whisking continuously until thickened and clear.

Facing page: BAVARIAN APPLE CAKE.

To serve, turn the cake out onto a serving dish and arrange a circle of sliced apple on top. Spoon over some of the sauce and serve the rest separately.

SERVES 6–8

WHITE AND DARK CHOCOLATE VELVET

This dessert is a chocolate lover's dream, and it's every bit as rich and smooth as its name suggests.

INGREDIENTS

DARK CHOCOLATE LAYERS

6 squares semi-sweet chocolate, grated □ $^1/_3$ cup unsalted butter □ 2 tbsps sugar □ 2 tbsps coffee □ ½ tbsp gelatin □ ½ cup sour cream □ 6 coconut macaroons □ 2 tbsps rum

WHITE CHOCOLATE LAYER

$^1/_3$ cup white chocolate, grated □ 2 tbsps milk □ 1 egg yolk, beaten □ 2 tbsps sugar □ ½ tbsp gelatin □ Water □ ½ cup sour cream □ Chocolate curls

Melt the dark chocolate in a double boiler and beat in the butter and sugar. Dissolve the gelatin in the coffee and stir into the chocolate mixture. Allow to cool, then fold in the sour cream. Spoon half the mixture into an oiled loaf pan and chill until set.

Crumble the macaroons and soak with rum. Sprinkle half in a layer on top of the dark chocolate layer and chill.

Melt the white chocolate with the milk in a double boiler. Allow to cool slightly and beat in the egg yolk and sugar. Dissolve the gelatin in 2 tbsps water and stir into the white chocolate mixture. When completely cool, fold in the sour cream. Allow to thicken and then spoon a layer on top of the macaroon layer. Chill until set.

Sprinkle the white chocolate with the remaining macaroons, and top with another layer of dark chocolate. Chill until completely set.

Loosen from the pan and turn out. Cut in slices to serve, and surround with chocolate curls.

COFFEE CREAMS WITH CHOCOLATE BRANDY SAUCE

The flavor of coffee makes chocolate taste even more 'chocolaty'. The creamy smooth textures of both the coffee custards and the sauce make this a really luxurious treat.

INGREDIENTS

½ cup strong coffee ☐ ½ cup cream ☐ 3 whole eggs ☐ 3 egg yolks
☐ 4 tbsps sugar

SAUCE

1 cup water ☐ ²/₃ cup sugar ☐ 4 squares semi-sweet chocolate
☐ 2 tbsps brandy

Heat the coffee and cream until almost boiling. Set aside.

Mix the eggs, egg yolks and sugar together until well blended but not frothy. Gradually mix in the coffee cream.

Pour the mixture into 6 dampened molds and place in a pan of warm water. The water should come halfway up the sides of the molds.

Bake in a preheated 350°F oven for 30 minutes or until set. Chill at least 2 hours.

To make the sauce, combine the water and sugar in a saucepan and heat to dissolve the sugar completely. Bring to the boil and cook rapidly for 5 minutes to make a clear syrup.

Chop the chocolate finely and add to the syrup. Stir until the chocolate melts smoothly. If necessary, heat the mixture gently. Add the brandy and allow to cool.

To serve, turn out the coffee creams onto serving plates and pour the chocolate sauce around the bases of each.

SERVES 6

Chapter 13

SWEET FANCIES

CREAM CHEESE BRULEE

A favorite pudding, this is made even tastier and creamier with the addition of cream cheese. Make sure the caramel is crisp before serving.

—————————— INGREDIENTS ——————————

½ cup light cream □ 1 tbsp fine granulated sugar □ 4 egg yolks □ ½ cup cream cheese □ ½ tsp almond extract □ Dark brown sugar

Scald the cream. Mix the fine granulated sugar and egg yolks together and pour on the cream gradually, mixing well. Whisk in the cream cheese, bit by bit, until completely incorporated.

Place the mixture over low heat in a heavy-based saucepan. Cook slowly, stirring constantly until the mixture thickens and coats the back of a spoon. Do not boil.

Add the almond extract and strain the mixture into a shallow heat-proof dish. Refrigerate until cold and set.

Sprinkle brown sugar evenly over the surface of the cold cheese custard and place under a moderate, preheated broiler until the sugar caramelizes. Allow to chill for 2 hours before serving.

FRUIT BRULEE

This is a quick version of crème brulée, but is as creamy and smooth as the original. The crunchy caramel topping is still there, and the addition of fruit lightens the richness.

—————————— INGREDIENTS ——————————

1 cup cream cheese □ 1 cup sour cream □ ¼ tsp vanilla extract □ 8oz strawberries, raspberries or blackberries □ Dark brown sugar

Facing page: CREAM CHEESE BRÛLÉE.

Beat the cream cheese until softened. Mix in the sour cream and vanilla.

Hull and slice the strawberries, if using. Place the fruit in individual heat-proof dishes and spoon over the cream cheese mixture. Chill several hours in the refrigerator.

Sprinkle the tops with an even layer of brown sugar, covering the cream cheese mixture completely. Place under a preheated moderate broiler until the sugar melts and caramelizes.

Place in the refrigerator again and chill until the sugar sets completely before serving.

SERVES 6

HONEYCOMB MOLD

This is a sweet, old-fashioned pudding revived for modern tastes. It's light and lovely froth on the bottom and a cool clear jelly on top. It separates like magic, all by itself!

--------------------------------- INGREDIENTS ---------------------------------

3 eggs, separated □ ¹/₃ cup fine granulated sugar □ Juice and rind of 2 lemons □ 1½ cups milk □ ½ cup cream □ 1 tbsp gelatin

Mix egg yolks and sugar together in a saucepan. Add the lemon rind pared in strips. Bring the milk and cream to the boil and pour gradually onto the eggs and sugar, whisking constantly.

Combine the gelatin and lemon juice and leave to soak. Cook the custard mixture over very low heat until the mixture coats the back of a spoon. Dissolve the gelatin over gentle heat and pour into the custard. Strain the mixture into a bowl and allow to cool.

Whisk the egg whites until stiff but not dry and fold into the custard. Pour the mixture into a lightly oiled 2 pint mold and chill until firm.

SERVES 6

Facing page: HONEYCOMB MOLD.

FRUIT SCONES

Scones filled with plump raisins or currants are a favorite on any tea table. Soured milk makes them rise higher, but if you don't happen to have any, make your own with a dash of lemon juice or vinegar.

───────── INGREDIENTS ─────────

1 cup milk ☐ 2 tsps lemon juice or vinegar ☐ 4 cups flour ☐ 2 tsps baking powder ☐ Pinch salt ☐ 4 tbsps butter or margarine ☐ 1 tbsp brown sugar ☐ 1 cup currants or raisins

Combine the milk and lemon juice or vinegar and leave to stand for about 10 minutes.

Sift the flour into a bowl with the baking powder and salt. Rub in the butter or margarine until the mixture resembles fine breadcrumbs. Stir in the brown sugar and fruit. Add the milk and mix well.

Turn out onto a floured surface and knead lightly until smooth. Roll out the dough to a thickness of 1 inch and cut into rounds with a floured 2½ inch cutter. Place on a warmed baking sheet and bake in a preheated 425°F oven for about 10 minutes or until risen and browned.

Serve warm with butter or clotted cream and jam.

GRIDDLE SCONES

Scones don't have to bake in the oven. They can be cooked on the heat of a griddle until they're light and tender. Mashed potatoes make a wonderfully rich dough.

───────── INGREDIENTS ─────────

1lb potatoes, cooked and mashed ☐ 2 tbsps butter or margarine ☐ 1 cup all-purpose flour ☐ Pinch salt ☐ Oil

Add butter to the potatoes and sift in the flour with a pinch of salt. Mix to form a soft dough.

Facing page: GRIDDLE SCONES.

Roll out on a floured surface and cut into triangles. Lightly oil a griddle or frying pan and place the scones on the hot surface. Cook 3 minutes per side or until golden brown and risen. Serve hot with butter.

MAKES 24

ORANGE BRANDY CAKE

A cake with the taste of fresh oranges and filled with brandy soaked fruit makes a marvelous treat at teatime. It keeps for days in an airtight container, and can be frozen un-iced.

INGREDIENTS

1½ cups golden raisins ◻ 4 tbsps brandy ◻ 2 oranges ◻ 1½ sticks butter or margarine ◻ ¾ cup sugar ◻ 3 eggs ◻ 2 cups all-purpose flour ◻ 1½ tbsps baking powder ◻ Pinch salt ◻ 2 cups powdered sugar

Place golden raisins in a bowl with the brandy. Grate the rind and squeeze the juice from one of the oranges and add. Cover and leave overnight to soak.

Cream the butter or margarine until soft. Beat in the sugar gradually until light. Beat in the eggs one at a time. If the mixture curdles, beat in a spoonful of flour. Sift in the rest with the baking powder and salt. Add soaked golden raisins and any liquid that hasn't been absorbed.

Pour the mixture into a 7 inch deep pan lined with oiled paper. Bake in a preheated 350°F oven for 1¼ hours or until a skewer inserted into the middle comes out clean. Cool in the pan briefly and then remove to a wire rack to cool completely.

To mix the icing, squeeze the juice from the remaining orange and sift in the powdered sugar. Mix well, adding hot water as necessary to make a spreadable icing. Peel the paper off the cake and spread over the icing. Allow to set before slicing to serve.

SERVES 8

Facing page: ORANGE BRANDY CAKE.

PINK SPARKLER

Add sparkle to jelly with pink champagne. A little bit of bubbly can turn a nursery sweet into a dessert for adults only.

INGREDIENTS

1½ cups water □ 1½ tbsps gelatin □ Juice and rind of 1 lemon □ ¾ cup sugar □ 1½ cups pink champagne

Pour ⅓ cup of the water into a saucepan and sprinkle over the gelatin. Leave for about 5 minutes to soak.

Add the rest of the water to the pan and dissolve over low heat. Add the lemon juice, rind and sugar and heat until almost boiling. Take off the heat and leave to stand for about 30 minutes.

Line a colander with a clean towel and place in a deep bowl. Pour the jelly into the colander and allow to drip through the towel. When all the jelly has dripped through, mix it with the champagne and pour into a dampened 3 cup mold. Chill until firmly set before turning out onto a plate to serve.

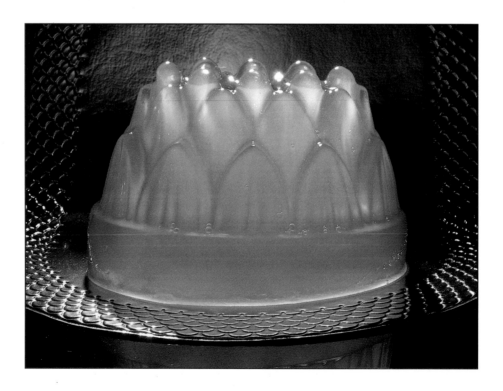

Above: PINK SPARKLER.

SOUFFLE CREPE CAKE

These are not ordinary pancakes. They are made with a light, puffy batter that is almost like a custard. They are superb on their own or filled with seasonal fruit.

―――――――――――― INGREDIENTS ――――――――――――

1½ cups milk □ ⅓ cup butter □ ¾ cup all-purpose flour □ ¾ cup powdered sugar □ 5 eggs, separated □ Flavoring extract □ Powdered sugar □ Fresh flowers and mint leaves to decorate

―――――――――――――――――――――――――――――――――――

Bring the milk to the boil and stir in the butter. Sift the flour and sugar into a bowl and beat in the egg yolks. Pour on the hot milk gradually, whisking constantly. The mixture may thicken slightly.

Whisk the egg whites until stiff and fold into the yolk mixture. Add vanilla, almond or rum flavoring. Heat a crêpe or omelet pan and add a bit of butter to coat the base. Spoon in some crêpe mixture and cook until the bottom is golden brown and the top just set. Stack browned side up on a serving plate.

Dust with powdered sugar and decorate with flours and mint leaves.

RAISIN BREAD

Two kinds of raisins, dark and golden, combine in this quick-to-mix tea bread that is as rich as a cake. It's delicious served warm spread with butter or cream cheese.

―――――――――――― INGREDIENTS ――――――――――――

1 stick butter or margarine □ ½ cup water □ ½ cup sugar □ 2 eggs, beaten □ 1 cup golden raisins □ 1 cup raisins □ 2 cups all-purpose flour □ 1 tbsp baking powder □ 2 tsp bicarbonate of soda □ Pinch salt □ 1 tsp ground ginger □ Oil

―――――――――――――――――――――――――――――――――――

Overleaf: RAISIN BREAD.

Melt the butter or margarine in a large saucepan. Stir in the water and sugar. Allow to cool slightly and then gradually beat in the eggs.

Stir in the golden raisins and raisins. Sift in the flour, baking powder, soda, salt and ginger. Mix all the ingredients together and pour into an oiled 10 × 4 inch loaf pan lined with a strip of oiled paper.

Bake in a preheated 350°F oven for about 45 minutes. Reduce the temperature to 300°F and bake a further 15 minutes. Allow to cool in the pan briefly and then place on a wire rack. Slice when still slightly warm or wrap in foil and reheat to serve.

SERVES 12

MINT TURKISH DELIGHT

This confectionery is one of the best after dinner treats. The texture of these sweets is divine and the minty taste makes a perfect finish to a meal.

INGREDIENTS

3 tbsps gelatin ☐ 1 cup water ☐ 2 cups granulated sugar ☐ 3 lemons ☐ 2 tbsps finely chopped fresh mint ☐ 2 cups fine granulated sugar ☐ 1 tbsp creme de menthe ☐ 2 tbsps cornstarch ☐ 2 tbsps powdered sugar

---

Sprinkle the gelatin on top of half of the water in a small saucepan. Place the rest of the water and the granulated sugar in a heavy-based pan and stir over low heat until the sugar is completely dissolved.

Bring the mixture to the boil and add the lemon juice and mint. Reduce the heat and simmer for about 5 minutes. Add the fine granulated sugar gradually, whisking constantly until completely dissolved. Boil again for about 5 minutes.

Add the creme de menthe and strain into a dampened shallow, rectangular pan. Allow to cool completely and then refrigerate overnight.

Sift the cornstarch and powdered sugar onto a cool work surface.

Above: Mint Turkish Delight.

Dip the pan into very hot water right up to the rim for a few seconds only. Turn the mixture out onto the work surface and cut into small squares. Toss in the cornstarch and powdered sugar mixture to coat evenly and leave to stand uncovered for about 1 hour for a crust to form. Store in an airtight container.

MAKES ABOUT 2lbs

CHOCOLATE AND RASPBERRY PROFITEROLES

Raspberries and chocolate are one of the world's best flavor combinations. This dessert uses them twice for a double treat.

INGREDIENTS

1 cup water □ 1 stick butter or margarine □ 1¼ cups all-purpose flour, sifted □ Pinch salt □ 4 eggs □ 6 squares unsweetened chocolate □ ½ cup sugar □ 1 cup water □ 2 tbsps raspberry liqueur □ 1 square semi-sweet chocolate □ 1½ cups heavy cream □ 8oz fresh raspberries □ Powdered sugar

---

Bring the water and butter or margarine slowly to the boil in a medium saucepan. Make sure that the fat has melted before the water comes up to the boil. Boil rapidly for a few seconds and then remove from the heat. Immediately add the sifted flour with a pinch of salt and beat until the mixture comes away from the sides of pan.

Spread the mixture out on a plate to cool. When cool to the touch, return to the pan and beat in the eggs one at a time. Beat well in between the addition of each egg. The mixture should be smooth and shiny, but hold its shape. All the eggs may not be needed, but try to use at least 3.

Pipe or spoon the mixture onto lightly oiled baking sheets in 1 inch mounds, leaving about 2 inches between each mound. Place in a pre-heated 425°F oven and bake for about 20–25 minutes or until risen and crisp. Slice in half and leave on a wire rack to cool.

Chop the unsweetened chocolate into small pieces and combine with the sugar and water in a small saucepan. Bring to the boil and then simmer for about 10 minutes or until thickened. Set aside to cool.

Melt the semi-sweet chocolate and allow to cool. Reserve ⅓ cup of the cream and whisk the remainder until soft. Fold in the cooled but still liquid chocolate.

Facing page: CHOCOLATE AND RASPBERRY PROFITEROLES.

Reserve about ¼ of the raspberries and fill the bottom half of each profiterole with the rest of the berries. Pipe or spoon on the chocolate cream. Place on the tops and sprinkle with powdered sugar.

Purée the reserved raspberries and sieve to remove the seeds. Stir the purée into the chocolate sauce and let down with water if necessary, as the sauce should not be too thick. Add the raspberry liqueur and spoon the sauce onto serving plates, coating the bases completely.

Place the filled profiteroles on each plate. Drizzle the reserved cream around the outside edge of the sauce. Use a knife or skewer to make a pattern in the cream and sauce. Serve immediately.

SERVES 6

ALMOND CREAMS

A smooth, creamy dessert is perfect any time of the year. This one is almondy and although rich tasting, is really light. Add fresh seasonal fruit, sliced and arranged around the base.

INGREDIENTS

1 cup milk □ 2 cups ground almonds □ ½ cup sugar □ 1 tbsp gelatin □ 4 tbsps water □ 1½ cups whipping cream □ Almond extract (optional) □ Toasted sliced almonds to decorate

Place the milk and ground almonds in a saucepan. Bring just to the boil and then remove from the heat. Stir in the sugar and leave the mixture to infuse for 30 minutes. Strain and return the milk to the rinsed out pan. Discard the almonds.

Soak the gelatin in the water for 5 minutes in a small saucepan. Dissolve it over low heat and pour into the almond milk. Set the pan in a bowl of ice water and stir constantly until the mixture thickens.

Remove from the ice water and whisk the cream until soft. Fold into the almond mixture. Taste and add almond extract, if desired. Pour into 8 lightly oiled molds or ramekins and chill until completely set.

Dip the molds or ramekins briefly into hot water to loosen the mixture and turn out onto serving plates. Decorate with the toasted almonds.

Facing page: ALMOND CREAMS.

THOUSAND LEAVES CAKE

A very impressive but easy-to-make pastry treat, this can be filled with fruit and cream or lemon curd as a change from the ricotta filling.

INGREDIENTS

1½lbs puff pastry □ 8oz ricotta cheese □ 4 tbsps sugar □ 1 cup heavy cream □ 3 tbsps rum □ 4 squares semi-sweet chocolate, chopped □ Powdered sugar

Roll out the pastry and cut four circles about 10 inches in diameter. Place on baking sheets and prick lightly with a fork.

Place in a preheated 400°F oven for about 8 minutes.

Beat the ricotta cheese and sugar with half of the cream until smooth. Whip the rest of the cream and fold in with the rum and chocolate.

Above and facing page: THOUSAND LEAVES CAKE.

When the pastry layers are cool, carefully spread the filling over three of them, reserving the best one for the top. Sprinkle thickly with powdered sugar.

SERVES 6–8

APRICOT ALMOND STRIPES

An apricot purée and an almond cream layered in stripes make this more than just another jelly. It also looks pretty in individual dessert glasses.

INGREDIENTS

1 cup dried apricots □ Lemon juice □ 1 tbsp gelatin □ 1 tbsp brandy (optional) □ 2 cups heavy cream □ $^1/_3$ cup sugar □ 4 egg yolks □ 1½ cups milk □ ¾ cup ground blanched almonds □ 1 tbsp Amaretto or 1 tsp almond extract

Place the apricots in a saucepan and cover with water. Add a dash of lemon juice and cook slowly until very soft. Add more water as necessary during cooking. Purée the fruit in a food processor and allow to cool.

Soak half of the gelatin in 2 tbsps water for about 5 minutes. Dissolve over gentle heat and pour into the apricot purée. Whip the cream lightly and fold half of it into the apricot purée. Add the brandy, if using.

Mix the egg yolks and the sugar together. Bring the milk to the boil and stir into the eggs and sugar. Place over low heat and cook until the mixture coats the back of a spoon. Soak the remaining gelatin in 2 tbsps of water and dissolve over gentle heat.

Stir the almonds and Amaretto or almond extract into the custard and pour in the gelatin. Allow to cool completely and then fold in remaining cream.

When the mixtures are nearly set, spoon them into an oiled 2½ cup mold, alternating the flavors. Alternatively, set in layers in dessert glasses. Chill until set.

Facing page: APRICOT ALMOND STRIPES.

STRAWBERRIES IN COINTREAU CREAM

When you need an instant pudding this can't be surpassed. It tastes every bit as good as it looks, too.

———————————— INGREDIENTS ————————————

1lb strawberries, hulled and washed □ 1 cup heavy cream □ 2 tbsps
Cointreau □ Fresh bay leaves to decorate

Drain the strawberries well and cut them in half.

Whip the cream until slightly thickened but still very soft. Fold in the Cointreau and spoon onto dessert plates.

Arrange the strawberries cut side down on the cream and decorate the plates with bay leaves. Serve immediately.

SERVES 6

ROSE GERANIUM ICE CREAM

The sweet, old-fashioned essence of roses flavors this smooth ice cream. The flowers are geraniums, though, and they come in lemon flavor, too.

———————————— INGREDIENTS ————————————

12 rose geranium leaves, washed □ 2 cups cream □ 8 egg yolks □ ½ cup
sugar □ 2 cups heavy cream, lightly whipped □ Geranium leaves and flowers
for decoration

Facing page: STRAWBERRIES IN COINTREAU CREAM.
Overleaf: ROSE GERANIUM ICE CREAM.

Bruise the leaves to release the flavor and place in a saucepan with the cream. Bring to the boil and then leave to infuse for about 15 minutes. Whisk the egg yolks and sugar and strain on the cream. Place over gentle heat and cook until the mixture coats the back of a spoon. Stir constantly and do not allow the mixture to boil.

Cool completely and then fold in the whipped cream. Place in an ice cream machine and follow the manufacturer's instructions or freeze in a deep tray until the sides are firm. Whisk to break up ice crystals. Freeze and whisk again before leaving to freeze solid.

To serve, remove the ice cream from the freezer at least 30 minutes before serving and place in the refrigerator. Scoop into serving dishes and garnish with leaves and flowers.

CRANBERRY ALMOND PUDDINGS

Cranberries, with their fresh taste and beautiful color, can be used in so many ways other than as a side dish for poultry. Try them in an almondy steamed pudding.

INGREDIENTS

1 stick butter or margarine □ ½ cup sugar □ 2 eggs, beaten □ ¾ cup all-purpose flour □ 1 tsp baking powder □ 4 tbsps ground almonds □ 4oz whole cranberry sauce □ 2 eggs, separated □ 2 tbsps sugar □ Grated rind of 1 lemon □ 2 tbsps Madeira

Beat the butter or margarine until very soft, and gradually beat in the sugar until the mixture is light and fluffy.

Add the beaten egg, a little at a time, whisking well in between each addition. If the mixture curdles, beat in a small amount of flour. Sift in the remaining flour and the baking powder. Add the almonds and fold into the egg mixture until well incorporated.

Butter or oil 6 small heat-proof molds and spoon a small amount of the cranberry sauce into the bottom of each. Use all the whole cranberries, reserving 2 tbsps of the liquid to use in the sauce.

Facing page: CRANBERRY ALMOND PUDDINGS.

Spoon the pudding mixture on top of the cranberries to within ½ inch of the top of the molds. Lightly grease small squares of foil and cover the top of each mold.

Tie securely, place the molds on a rack above boiling water and steam for about 30 minutes. Top up the water as necessary during cooking. The puddings are done when a skewer inserted into the center of the puddings comes out clean. Leave to stand in the molds while making the sauce.

Beat the egg yolks, sugar and lemon rind together in the top of a double boiler until the mixture is thick and mousse-like. Add the reserved cranberry liquid and the Madeira. Place over barely simmering water and whisk until the mixture is light and fluffy.

Do not allow the water under the mixture to boil, or let the mixture to get too hot. Take it off the heat while whisking the egg whites until stiff but not dry. Fold into the yolk mixture.

To serve, unmold the puddings onto dessert plates and spoon the sauce around them.

ICED COCONUT FRUIT SQUARES

Just the thing with hot tea, these pastries have a delectable chewy filling with lots of coconut, fruit and nuts, all topped off by an almond flavored icing.

INGREDIENTS

1½ cups all-purpose flour □ Pinch salt □ ⅓ cup butter, margarine or lard □ Water

FILLING

½ cup desiccated coconut □ ½ cup candied cherries □ ½ cup walnuts □ ½ cup golden raisins □ ½ cup currants □ 2 tbsps sugar □ 2 tbsps butter, melted □ 1 egg beaten

ICING

2 cups powdered sugar □ Hot water □ Almond extract

Facing page: ICED COCONUT FRUIT SQUARES.

Sift the flour and salt into a bowl, rub in the fat until the mixture resembles fine breadcrumbs. Add enough water to make a firm dough. Roll out and line a shallow 8 × 12 inch pan with the dough.

Mix the coconut, fruit and nuts with the sugar, butter and egg. Pour onto the pastry and spread out. Bake in a preheated 375°F oven for 25 minutes or until golden.

Mix enough water into the powdered sugar to make a pourable icing. Add almond extract. Pour over the fruit filling while still warm and leave to set. Cut into squares when cool.

SERVES 12

FRUIT AND WALNUT TART

Sweet shortcrust pastry filled with a fruit and walnut mixture makes up this unbelievably rich pastry. A dash of whiskey reveals its Scottish ancestry.

INGREDIENTS

1 cup all-purpose flour □ Pinch salt □ 4 tbsps butter or margarine □ 1 egg, beaten □ 2–4 tbsps water

FILLING

4 tbsps butter □ 4 tbsps sugar □ 1 egg □ 1 cup candied fruit □ 1 cup golden raisins □ 1 cup walnuts □ 1 tbsp whiskey

Sift the flour with a pinch of salt into a bowl or process in a food processor. Rub in the butter or margarine until the mixture resembles fine bread-crumbs or process once or twice. Work in the egg and enough water to make a firm but pliable dough.

Roll out and line an 8 inch flan dish, reserving the trimmings.

Combine butter and sugar until light and soft, then beat in the egg. Stir in the fruit, walnuts and whiskey. Pour into the pastry case and use the remaining pastry to make a lattice top. Bake in a preheated 375°F oven for about 25 minutes or until golden brown.

Facing page: FRUIT AND WALNUT TART.

INDEX